Voices of Wellness
A Mental Health Anthology

Candice Hayes | Shawnti Refuge | DaVonda St. Clair | Dr. Carrie Young-McWilliams | Shakira Releford | Dr. Cheryl Cooper | Bridgette Nelson | Elona Washington | Dr. Azuré Smith-Swan

Copyright © 2024 by The Author's Journey
All rights reserved.

No part of this publication may be reproduced, distributed, or transmitted in any form or by any means, including photocopying, recording, or other electronic or mechanical methods, without the prior written permission of the publisher, except as permitted by U.S. copyright law. For permission requests, contact info@theauthorsjourney.co..

For privacy reasons, some names, locations, and dates may have been changed.

Book Cover by Daniel O

2nd edition 2024

Contents

CHAPTER 1 | CANDICE HAYES _____ 1
Candles of Hope: Lighting the Way for Mental Health Support_____

CHAPTER 2 | SHAWNTI REFUGE   ERROR! BOOKMARK NOT DEFINED.
From Breakdown to Breakthrough _____

CHAPTER 3 | DAVONDA ST. CLAIR _____ 183
Unbroken Brilliance: From Shadows to Strength _____

CHAPTER 4 | DR. CARRIE YOUNG-MCWILLIAMS _____ 55
Misread Minds: A Battle with Anxiety and Mood Adjustment Disorder _____

CHAPTER 5 | SHAKIRA RELEFORD _____ 555
What We Know About OCD is Dead Wrong _____

CHAPTER 6 | DR. CHERYL COOPER _____ 98
No Dark-Skinned Woman, You are Not the Same as Her _____

CHAPTER 7 | BRIDGETTE NELSON _____ 9821
Suppression of the High-Functioning Black Woman_____

CHAPTER 8 | ELONA WASHINGTON _____ 121
Searching for Safety: Piecing Together a Shattered Past_____

CHAPTER 9 | DR. AZURÉ SMITH-SWAN, LCSW, CFSW _____ 1389
Ascending the Staircase: The Therapist in the Chair _____

NATIONAL HELPLINES AND RESOURCES _____ 18080

LET'S STAY IN TOUCH _____ 1833

Foreword

What if, in this season, your strength isn't measured by how much you have endured and can hold on to, but by what you have the courage to let go of or walk away from?

In the beautifully complex areas of our lives, we are often propelled by a societal force that measures success in material gains. We chase accolades and possessions, often losing sight of our true values, our well-being, and our peace. We strive to exceed the accomplishments of those who came before us, all while carrying the unexamined traumas of our ancestors, not realizing these burdens are part of our journey. As we bury the pains of our pasts in pursuit of titles, degrees, marriages, homes, and careers, we often don't see that we are merely surviving. When our love and life spring from a place of survival, it's too easy to compromise not only our physical health but also our mental and spiritual peace at the end of it all.

But what if we chose to pause the relentless advance of society's clock? What if we turned our attention to the often-neglected realms of mental and spiritual health? What if, instead of just surviving, we decided to surrender? To release all the pain and hurt that has negatively fueled our ambitions and start achieving from a place of peace and intention? Imagine stepping off the relentless treadmill of external validations and societal expectations. Envision a life where success isn't about survival but about living intentionally and achieving from a place of peace. What if you could reach new heights not to silence the doubters or to heal old wounds, but to fulfill your deepest aspirations for your defined place of purpose and calm?

Here, in these musings, we begin to find the delicate balance of our inner lives, where true fulfillment lies.

This anthology stands as a guiding light for those braving the turbulent waters of mental wellness. It is a collection that not only witnesses our struggles but also celebrates the profound moments of self-discovery and healing that define our resilience. Each narrative within these pages taps into the fears and hopes of diverse individuals, offering a path of self-love marked by both trials and triumphs.

Through these stories and essays, we invite you to explore the myriad ways in which we reclaim our strength and redefine healing and success on our own terms. These reflections serve as a lens through which to view the struggles many of us face alone, reminding us of the collective empathy, understanding, and support that can arise from our shared human experiences.

More than a collection of texts, this anthology is a dialogue between souls, a whispered encouragement in moments of doubt, and a vibrant celebration in times of triumph. As you turn each page, may you find not just solace and understanding but also the courage to embrace and shape your path toward healing freely.

Together, let's embark on this next chapter with open hearts and minds, ready to learn, to feel, and ultimately, to show up in this world authentic and whole. It is my hope that you connect with these stories, see reflections of your own journey, and feel empowered to take the steps necessary for your newfound restoration and peace—not just because you deserve this, but because we have been waiting for you. We need you in the right place, with the right mind. You are enough.

Yours in wellness,

Rochelle M. Thompson, PsyD, LL.M., SHRM-SCP
CEO, RMThompson & Company, LLC | www.rochellemthompson.com

Chapter 1 | Candice Hayes

Candles of Hope
Lighting the Way for Mental Health Support

**Trigger Warning: This chapter discusses suicide and may not be suitable for all readers.

> *To be a Black woman and mother is to be a warrior for love and justice.*
> —Unknown

At 19 years old, I was a single mother of two and lived at home with my parents when my father got a phone call from a young man he did not know. It was Jarius calling for my father's permission to take me out. Jarius told me later that he dreamt about me, which was weird because we'd only seen each once. It was during Bible study, and we never exchanged words. But a year later, he called our pastor asking for my number. And it was our pastor who suggested he speak with my father.

When we dated, Jarius played tight end at the University of North Alabama, and the day before NFL draft day, we got married at the courthouse. The Arizona Cardinals drafted him in the 7th round, blessing our family in more ways than one. I immediately got pregnant; and we had a boy, Caleb. I loved being a wife and mother, and being an NFL wife wasn't too bad either! I was born and raised middle-class in Alabama but relocating to Arizona, we lived a whole new lifestyle. I got to meet different kinds of people, the big-time players, and was treated like a celebrity's wife everywhere I went. We got to shop at exclusive places, and they would even open the shop a little early to accommodate us. While it was fun, my dad taught us to never forget where we came from and to remain humble; so we did.

Jarius and I have been married for 27 years, and from day one, he accepted my children as his own. As our baby boy grew, we noticed he started to struggle emotionally around 14 years old. He also started to have debilitating migraines, he'd stay in his room during family events, and decline traveling. We took him to the doctor, and they prescribed medication for his migraines, but it didn't help.

When he turned 19, he had difficulty sleeping at night and the headaches got worse. One night, Jarius and I heard a gurgling sound coming from his room. It sounded like he was gasping for air, so we ran to his room to help. Caleb was crying and told us to tell Kendall I love him. He thought he was dying. I called 911, and we sat and prayed over him until they arrived. By the time the EMT got there, it had passed. The next day, though, the same thing happened. We tried to help, but he just stood like a statue in the kitchen, looking up at the ceiling. It was like he was hallucinating. Then, without any warning, he ran out of the house yelling, "I can't take this anymore!" For a split second, we just stared at each other, frightened, then Jarius ran out of the house after him. A few minutes later, he came back inside and said, "I can't catch him. I can't even find him." This only increased our worry, so we did what every Black parent knows better to do. We called the police. My voice shaking, I told the officer, "He's wearing a hoodie, and yes, he's a Black male. Caleb has never been in trouble before. He's not on drugs. He's just having a mental breakdown."

My heart was racing, and all I could do was pray. I'd asked the Alabama police department to find and return my son safely. I had to forego the centuries of beatings, lynchings, racial profiling, etc. and trust that these officers would not harm my boy. This was during the time they were stereotyping Black men for wearing hoodies. This was following Philando Castille and a handful of other innocent black men's senseless deaths. What else was there to do? We didn't know if Caleb would return on his own. And we prayed to God that he didn't run off to hurt himself.

The officers found him a few moments later in a wooded area, walking calmly, and thankfully, they did so without overreacting. But instead of bringing him home, they called an ambulance to have him sent to the hospital — actually, the psych ward. It was his first visit to a psychiatric facility. I was gut-punched and a new level of fear, worry, and guilt arose. He'd never been away from home before. If he left the house, it was to visit his brother and sister. In my mind, I pictured Caleb in a room by himself, lonely. I started thinking that I could have sought more help for him sooner. I should have seen this coming. I should have stopped it. It's my job as a mom to take care of my boy. And I failed.

After two weeks in the hospital, Caleb returned home. The medications prescribed by the doctors allowed Caleb to function, but he was never the laughing little boy he was before the headaches. We accepted that he didn't like to be around other people, so we altered our lives to suit him. That meant no more family vacations. I also made it a point to always stay close to home. We didn't want our family members to have to take care of him if something happened. There were times when my mom would take him so Jarius and I could spend time together, but all in all, we made sure we were always with Caleb.

During all of this, I found a hobby: candle-making. I'd been buying candles from the popular stores, but when I lit them, I always got a headache; it didn't matter the brand or scent. But I loved the relaxation it brought, so I started researching how to make my own. Kim Braud's Fleurty Wick Candle Company offered a candle-making course, so I drove to Atlanta to enroll. I set up a candle-making studio in the back of my home and started giving them to friends and family. I also owned Candy's Corporate Cleaning and would give candles as gifts for my clients. I've been an entrepreneur for more than 16 years, and I enjoyed the fusion of my work and hobby. Working for myself also meant that I had the freedom and flexibility to look after Caleb. And by the grace of God, it was my schedule's flexibility that saved my son's life.

CANDLES OF HOPE

Candy's Candles is the name I chose when my hobby turned into a business. I was doing really well, had a lot of loyal customers, and easily balanced both businesses. One day, Caleb and I were home alone, and my husband was at work about 15 minutes away. I was thinking about doing some work on my own and was about to head off to a client's location when I felt a strong urge to stay home. Obedient, I stayed home to work in my candle studio.

Like all mothers, some random thought crossed my mind, so I headed to Caleb's room to ask him a question. The house was quiet as usual, but as I got closer to the door, I started to hear a chilling, choking sound. I'd never heard that sound before — it was nothing like the sound Jarius and I had heard years before. It was horrible. Like he was almost at the end.
I was scared… I didn't know what I would find — or maybe I did. I'm sure, dear reader, you know too.

I opened the door. My fear was true. Panic hit me. My heart raced as I flew into supermommy mode and untied him. To this day, I'm unable to describe how I did it. Yet those sounds are forever etched in my memory. This is something I can't get out of my head. It doesn't matter how busy I am. I could be having a good day, then bam — the memory returns — knowing he didn't want to go on with life is hard. I tried. Jarius tried. To get him the best medical care. We changed our lives to make him comfortable. And he still didn't want to be here.

"Caleb! Why would you do this!" I picked him up and took him to the car. Caleb never resisted. I put my baby boy in the back seat. I prayed over him, assuring him that everything was going to be okay. He never looked at me. He didn't cry. He was just there.

At only 5 feet tall, I managed to get my 6-foot, 160-pound baby boy out of the car and to his brother's front door. After ringing the bell several times, he finally opened the door. When he saw us standing there, I could tell he knew something was horribly wrong. There were burns along Caleb's neck, and I'm sure my hair and clothes were disheveled. I didn't have the strength to keep up the Black Supermom façade; I felt frightened, confused, and vulnerable — emotions I'd never let my children see. Before saying hello, I blurted out, "Caleb just tried to kill his self!" Then I cried uncontrollably.

Heading to my oldest son's house, I kept trying to reach my husband at work, but he wasn't available. Fortunately, my son lived only 10 minutes away, but the drive felt endless. Unable to reach my husband, I sent a group text to my mother, sister, and daughter, letting them know what happened and inviting them to meet us at my son's house. Still, I have no idea how I was able to do all that. My hands were shaking. I was panicking and crying. All I knew was that I was going to do whatever it took to keep my son safe.

The ping from an incoming text message caused me to look down at my phone. Maybe my husband was finally trying to reach me. But it was my mother, a retired social worker, who replied, "This was a cry for help." I was overwhelmed by more panic and a crippling sense of failure as a parent. I let my son down. As his mom, I should have kept him safe. But I didn't. I failed at being a good parent. How could this be happening? Jarius finally called me back, and when I told him what happened, he rushed to Kendall's house. Together, we took him to the hospital. Caleb had told us before that he hated staying at the facility. But when his dad told him he had to go back, he said okay. Caleb never wanted to stay away from home, but even after what had happened, he knew he needed help.

When we arrived, there were no beds available in the psych ward, so they laid him down on a stretcher in the hallway of the ER. It was a horrendous experience for us all, especially having to relay the story multiple times to several different doctors. We stayed in the waiting room as long as we could, but eventually we had to head home. I cried like a baby. Every time we had to leave him, I cried. Days passed before they moved Caleb to the psych ward. I pray for a better outcome every time. Pray for healing, for transformation, and for restoration.

My daughter's upcoming wedding was just two weeks away. As I tried to shift my focus to wedding planning, I was caught up in conflicting emotions. On one hand, I wanted to be fully present and excited for my daughter, and I desperately wanted to share in her joy and happiness. However, the weight of my son's struggle hung heavy on my heart. I couldn't help but feel guilty for feeling happy while he was in the psychiatric ward. It felt like a betrayal.

A wave of guilt overcame me immediately when I caught myself smiling or laughing while discussing wedding details. How could I allow myself to feel happiness when my son was suffering? The Black Supermom cape was back on, so no one saw my struggles.

I did find joy when Caleb was discharged in time to attend the wedding. My husband and I were worried about what he would do. To our relief, he was able to participate, but the joy was short-lived. The wedding reception was marred by a food poisoning outbreak that landed several guests, including my husband, my late father, older son, and my niece, in the hospital. After this incident, Caleb was transferred to a restrictive 21-day facility. The limited visits and calls were agonizing, and I couldn't imagine what was going through my 19-year-old son's mind. When we met with the doctor, I was devastated to learn that Caleb would need medication for the rest of his life to manage his mental health condition.

My husband and I became Caleb's full-time caregivers, rearranging our schedules to ensure Caleb's needs were met. We missed out on vacations, family events, and other opportunities, as Caleb would often get anxious in social situations. It took an emotional and physical toll on me, leading to weight gain and hair loss.

Right before the holidays in 2022, Caleb made another attempt. This time, he was in the garage, and Jarius was able to prevent it. We took him back to the hospital, and after talking with the doctors, we made the decision to transfer him to a live-in facility. Caleb could receive the care and supervision he needed to thrive. When we dropped him off, he was okay with it. He even admitted that he knew he'd be safer there. At this facility, he's free to come and go, and we see him regularly. As a matter of fact, he calls me ALL the time, so I miss him, but not as much as I did when he was in the psych ward, and I definitely worry less. There are times when he confesses that he wants to come home. Then he stops and says, "No." He doesn't want to risk harm to himself. Jarius and I tell him he's welcome to come home whenever he wants. We don't ever want our boy to feel unwelcome.

LIGHTING THE WAY FOR MENTAL HEALTH SUPPORT

Throughout this journey, my husband and I remained silent, not sharing our struggles with friends and family due to the stigma surrounding mental illness. It was a lonely and painful journey, filled with self-doubt and questions about my abilities as a mother. However, I knew I had to be strong for my son and keep pushing forward.

A lot of marriages end because of the strain. However, this brought me and Jarius closer. Yes, it would have been much easier to throw in the towel, but our communication improved, and we worked together to take care of our son and each other. We couldn't leave the house for more than an hour without Caleb calling to check on us. When we wanted to have private conversations about anything, Caleb would come into the room.

This experience motivated me to create The Hope Journal and Hope Collection as a way to help other caregivers and individuals dealing with mental health challenges find an outlet for their emotions and a sense of relief. I hope that by breaking my silence and sharing my story, I can inspire others and help to break the stigma surrounding mental illness in our culture. It's my desire to:
- Break the silence: My husband and I initially remained silent about our struggles due to the stigma surrounding mental illness.

However, we realize the importance of sharing our story to inspire others and help break the stigma in our culture.
- Create resources for support: The Hope Journal and Hope Collection serve as outlets for caregivers and individuals dealing with mental health challenges to process emotions and find relief.
- Promote self-care: As the owner of Candy's Candles, my focus is to create products that promote self-care and mental wellness using eco-friendly and vegan materials for a serene atmosphere.
- Empower others: By sharing my story and creating resources, the goal is to empower other caregivers and help them realize they are not alone.
- Advocate for mental health awareness: Through my affiliations with various organizations, I am actively working to raise awareness and provide support for those affected.

Because mental health challenges can impact individuals and families from all walks of life, regardless of their financial status or social standing, this journey serves as a reminder that we are all vulnerable to mental health struggles, and it is critical to break the stigma surrounding these issues and provide support and resources for those affected, no matter their background.

CANDICE HAYES

Candice Hayes is a resilient and inspiring entrepreneur, mental health advocate, and NFL wife of a retired player who turned her personal struggles into a powerful platform for change. Married for 27 years, Candice and her husband have three adult children, one son-in-law, and three grandchildren. Her life took an unexpected turn when her youngest son, Caleb, was diagnosed with a mental health condition seven years ago.

As a mother, Candice faced the challenges of navigating the mental healthcare system while trying to maintain a sense of normalcy for her family. She and her husband took on the role of full-time caregivers for Caleb, adapting their lives to meet his needs. The experience was emotionally and physically taxing, but Candice remained determined to support her son.

Candice's entrepreneurial background includes a successful janitorial business, Candy's Corporate Cleaning, serving a diverse clientele. Her love for cleaning and organization even led her to write a handbook, "We Cleaned Our Home Yesterday," available on Amazon. Additionally, Candice founded Candy's Candles, a woman-owned business specializing in eco-friendly, vegan candles, wax melts, and room sprays that promote self-care and mental wellness.

Motivated by her personal journey, Candice created The Hope Journal and Hope Collection to provide resources and support for caregivers and individuals facing mental health challenges. She aims to break the stigma surrounding mental illness by sharing her story and empower others to seek help and practice self-care.

Candice's dedication to mental health advocacy extends beyond her businesses. She serves on the executive board of the North Alabama Black Realist Association of Huntsville, Alabama (Nareb), is a member of The Off the

Field NFL Wives Association and is involved with the Huntsville Metro Black Chamber of Commerce.

Through her resilience, compassion, and commitment to making a difference, Candice Hayes has become a voice of hope for countless individuals and families affected by mental illness, reminding them that they are not alone in their struggles.

For those who want to stay connected with Candice Hayes, you can easily find her on social media. Check out her Facebook page at Candice H Hayes and follow her on Instagram @CandiceHayes. If you're interested in non-toxic candles, room sprays, and cleaning sprays, make sure to visit her website at www.candyscandles.com.

For any inquiries or to start a conversation, feel free to drop an email at conversationwithcandice@gmail.com.

Stay connected and explore the world of non-toxic products with Candice.

REFLECTION QUESTIONS

1. The author mentions feelings of guilt for experiencing happiness while her son was struggling. How can caregivers cope with conflicting emotions and give themselves permission to find moments of positivity amidst difficult circumstances?

REFLECTION QUESTIONS

2. How can caregivers prioritize self-care while also providing support to a loved one with mental health challenges? What strategies or activities could help maintain balance and prevent burnout?

_____

_____

_____

_____

_____

_____

_____

_____

_____

_____

_____

_____

_____

REFLECTION QUESTIONS

3. In what ways can open communication and a strong partnership between partners help when facing the challenges of supporting a family member with mental illness? How can couples work together to navigate this difficult journey?

Chapter 2 | Shawnti Refuge

From Breakdown to Breakthrough

Mental health IS health, and my goal is to help have it not be stigmatized any longer.

—Shawnti Refuge

INTRODUCTION

I don't know about you, but I grew up in a society where we didn't tell our business to strangers. What went on in the house stayed in the house. After all, how can someone who doesn't know you help you solve your problems? As a Black girl growing up in a lower middle-class community, we also never saw psychiatrists or therapists because that was "white people shit."

I had a nervous breakdown at 41 and overcame it holistically. I've had experiences throughout my life, and certain choices led me there. The definition of a nervous breakdown is a condition in which someone can no longer function normally in their daily lives. It usually occurs because of extreme stress.

MIRROR, MIRROR ON THE WALL

Imagine looking in the mirror and not recognizing yourself.

Imagine having emotional outbursts, yelling, and screaming at people for no reason. Your whole body is full of rage, and you have no power to control it. The littlest things tick you off.

I was being mean as f*ck to my wife. Hell, I was mean to everybody — the kids, the dog, EVERYBODY. I clocked hours staying in the house so I could avoid people. I wanted to be isolated in every sense of the word. I didn't wanna talk to anybody. If I was talking to them, it wasn't pretty. When I went off on someone, it got really bad.

I could literally picture another version of myself sitting on a sofa behind me and just watching me go off on whoever I was going off on. It was weird, and I didn't like it. The person sitting on the couch was just watching me act crazy and didn't try to stop me. She was just looking at me and shaking her head as if I were embarrassing her, and she pitied me. The person sitting on that couch, looking at me, was the real me.

I knew I was sad, but I didn't know what to do about it other than pray, so I stayed praying. I was praying, pretending, avoiding, and denying until one Sunday in 2018, when I woke up and immediately did not feel well emotionally. It felt like I had a dark cloud hanging over my head, literally. I went on with my day, feeling sad but pushing through, thinking that this funk would pass.

Throughout the day, I was uncontrollably crying until I started to feel mad and upset. I was lashing out and talking crazy to people, and I knew this was not me. After about a month of acting this way, Angela finally told me that I needed to see someone because she did not know how much longer she would be able to take me through these uncontrollable mood swings. I took that as her telling me that she would leave me, so the very next day, I got online and scheduled an appointment to see my family doctor. I didn't know where else to turn, so I started with her.

Later, I could feel that my verbal outbursts were going to turn physical because I was picturing myself harming people. I never once had the urge to harm myself. It was just other people I wanted to harm. One person in particular, my ex's partner, had been harassing me through phone calls and texts. Things had gotten so bad that I pictured myself knocking on their door, waiting for them to answer, and when they did, I would be standing there in a black hoodie, pointing a gun in their face, and capping off. This was what scared me. I'm a lover, not a fighter — especially not a killer.

I'M NOT CRAZY

I told my family doctor about my mood swings and the uncontrollable crying. She said that I might be a little depressed, and she gave me a low dose of antidepressants. Keep in mind that I'd already been down this road, and they didn't work, but I wasn't opposed to trying them again and taking them for a longer period of time. I took the antidepressants for six weeks and went back to her office to tell her how it was going.

I said, "This sh*t ain't working."

She chuckled and replied, "Maybe you need a stronger dose. I'll up the dose, and you come back in six weeks and let me know how you feel."

She had been my doctor for a very long time, so I wasn't going to go against what she suggested because I trusted her. I took the higher dose of antidepressants for six weeks and reported again, "This shit ain't working."

She looked at me and said, "I'm not saying anything's wrong with you, but I need you to go see a psychiatrist."

All I'm thinking is, "Psychiatrist! Black people don't go see psychiatrists. That's white people sh*t."

I pictured myself lying on some white lady's couch, telling her about all my issues, and she was just writing and looking at me, judging me, and handing me more drugs. That's exactly what happened, minus the judging part.

After speaking with the psychiatrist, she prescribed me a higher dose of antidepressants. She told me to take them for 30 days and come back to let her know how they were working. I took them faithfully every day for 30 days.

Within the first few days, I started feeling better; I wasn't crying or having outbursts. I took the meds for the next 30 days as prescribed. I thought I was getting better. On the 31st day, I had an appointment with the psychiatrist to go back to see her and get more meds.

On the 31st day, the medications stopped working! I was back on the roller coaster ride of crying, anger, sadness, and withdrawal. This was when I decided that I didn't want to spend the rest of my life controlling my emotions with medication. The psychiatrist advised me to get a therapist.

BLACK PEOPLE DON'T SEE THERAPISTS

As much as I didn't want to see a psychiatrist, I *really* didn't want to see a therapist, but I went anyway. I looked for a Black woman and finally found one who was kind of an older lady. She was close to my job, so I could easily go there and come back during the day.

The first session was fine, considering that was my first time going to therapy. We talked about what was happening to me, and she said we were going to work on a plan so that I could overcome the issues I was having.

At that time, I told her some confessions that I had never made to anyone in my life. She didn't offer me any help; she was just listening. I had weekly appointments with her, but it didn't dawn on me at the time that I wasn't leaving better than when I came. I had gotten to feel like I was just telling her my business, and she was just taking it all in.

So, I found another therapist. She was also Black, but she was a little younger — not too young because I didn't want to feel like I was talking to a little girl. I made an appointment. I talked to this therapist for the initial consultation. For the next appointment, I never heard from her again.

At first, I thought she forgot about me because, at the time, her business was in the process of moving to a new office location. I gave her a few weeks, then I contacted her again to set an appointment. After so many tries, I concluded that she ghosted me.

For any therapist reading this, if you feel you and your potential client would not work well together, please let them know. Professionally, you could tell the person that you don't feel that you are a good fit for them and suggest that they turn to someone else. Ghosting someone who is coming to you for help is not good for that person's mental health.

I started thinking back to my past relationships and thinking they always left me. My first girlfriend and my second girlfriend both left me. I had it in my mind that they always leave me, and it was a matter of time before my wife would leave me, too.

I realized that I had abandonment issues.

Luckily, I found another therapist who was also near my job that I could go to on my lunch break. She was Black, not too old or too young. I went to her, letting her know what my issues were and how I found her. I told her that I didn't expect to see her for long because people always leave me.

We began talking about my childhood. I admit I was very standoffish with her because she was a stranger, and I was always told not to talk to strangers about my business. At this point, I had no choice because I needed help.

What Goes on in the House Stays in the House

After weeks of therapy and a diagnosis of severe depression and anxiety, I finally let her into my life so that she could see what it was like and where I came from. She had me start off with journaling. I was against it because, again, I thought journaling was for white people. I had in mind that black people didn't discuss their problems; they just worked through them. They damn sure didn't write about it because somebody would find it, read it, and go tell someone else about it.

For example, back in middle school, my friend and I were writing notes to each other and keeping them in a box. My friend's mom found the box and opened a letter that I wrote, which was about me having sex with one of my boyfriends. Her mom was a nurse and called me out immediately, asking me if I was having sex.

I was scared of my friend's mom, so I said no. I was even more scared that she would tell my mama, so every time she asked me, I kept saying no. She kept saying I wasn't going to get in trouble, but I needed to get protection. I still said no. Everyone found out I was lying because I got pregnant shortly after. I was 14.

My therapist assured me that journaling would be a way to help me revisit my past and face things that I had in the past so that I could heal from them. Initially, when I started journaling, I disliked it because it made me mad to have to revisit all of those bad times. So, at my next appointment, I told her, and she showed me another way to journal, called guided journaling. Guided journaling is when you answer a specific set of questions and record the answers in a notebook. I was digging the guided journaling, so I began doing that every day.

After about a week, I started feeling better, and I couldn't believe it. I was able to talk about my childhood abuse in therapy. I was able to talk about my relationship with my mother. I was able to talk about middle school, how I didn't have any friends, and how I thought no one liked me. I was able to talk about being a teen mom and its effect on me. I had no clue back then but being 14 and a teen mom was a form of trauma. I was able to talk about what I did to my second child's father. I talked about my relationship with my second daughter. I talked about my affair.

It took me a year of therapy to be able to face, acknowledge, and essentially begin the healing process. The healing process for me also meant speaking to my children and my wife.

I have rekindled my relationship with my oldest daughter as of this chapter's writing. There was an attempt to at least talk with my youngest daughter, but it did not work out well. I invited her to attend therapy sessions with me, but she never responded. I'm not opposed to rekindling our relationship; however, she will have to make the next move.

Through therapy and guided journaling, I was able to look inside and fix myself. The healing process is a journey that I take every day.

SHAWNTI REFUGE

Shawnti Refuge, CEO of Shawnti Refuge Journals, is a certified mental health coach, mental health advocate, keynote speaker, and author. She supports women in releasing, healing, and living their best lives through guided journaling. Shawnti believes in shedding emotional baggage by addressing its root causes and facilitating natural healing. Inspired by her own experiences and mental health challenges, she has created a series of self-care-guided journals. Shawnti's mission is to offer a safe space for healing through guided journaling.

Born in Beaumont, TX, Shawnti now resides in the Houston suburbs with her wife, Angela, and is a proud mother of three adult children. When she's not crafting journals, Shawnti enjoys reading, binge-watching TV shows, and cherishing moments with her family and friends. Currently, she's penning a book based on her personal wellness journey.

Shawnti Refuge Journals is dedicated to empowering individuals who recognize the vital role journaling plays in self-care. Advocating self-love, self-awareness, and self-care through guided journaling, she creates journals that enhance emotional, physical, mental, spiritual, and financial well-being.

https://www.shawntirefuge.com

REFLECTION QUESTIONS

1. The author tried several therapists before finding one they felt comfortable with. What qualities or approaches would you look for in a therapist to ensure a good therapeutic fit? How important is representation/shared identities?

_____

_____

_____

_____

_____

_____

_____

_____

_____

_____

_____

_____

_____

REFLECTION QUESTIONS

2. Healing from trauma, depression, and other mental health challenges is described as a non-linear journey. How can we develop self-compassion for the setbacks and difficulties inevitable in that journey?

_____

_____

_____

_____

_____

_____

_____

_____

_____

_____

_____

_____

REFLECTION QUESTIONS

3. What are the potential benefits and risks of being open about mental health struggles to destigmatize the experience? How can we create safe spaces to share these stories?

Chapter 3 | DaVonda St. Clair

Unbroken Brilliance
From Shadows to Strength

**Trigger Warning: This chapter discusses sexual assault and may not be suitable for all readers.

> *I can be changed by what happens to me, but I refuse to be reduced by it.*
>
> —Dr. Maya Angelou

MARKS OF MEMORY: ECHOES OF THE ASSAULT

My body moved slowly, each step loaded with the weight of last night's brutality. As a military member, calling in sick wasn't straightforward; so, I pushed myself to go to work, my face bearing subtle yet painful evidence of violence — bruises marking my face and body, a busted lip, and an eye marooned by burst blood vessels around my pupil. Throughout the morning, I kept my head down, focused intently on my computer screen, doing everything to avoid eye contact with co-workers and people walking through the office, keeping my mind busy trying to keep from replaying the horrors from the day before, fighting back tears.

The unexpected call to the First Sergeant's office sent a surge of anxiety through me. Sitting angled in front of their desk in an attempt to hide my injuries, the First Sergeant's voice broke through my attempts at composure as he disclosed his awareness of the incident and asked what happened. Describing the assault was excruciating; my voice faltered as I recounted how someone I had trusted and dated for two years became my assailant — his knee in my back, the tight grip around my neck as I gasped for air, his hand smashing me face first into the mattress, then smashing my face on the floor. The visible blue and purple bruises around my neck peeked out from under my uniform collar, bearing mute testimony to the savage violence.

The First Sergeant directed me immediately to the hospital. Arriving at the hospital, I was met with people and an environment that, for the first time that day, made me feel less anxious but safe. The nurse's gentle approach provided a small comfort as she explained the procedures ahead — a physical assault exam and treatment for physical trauma. The examination was thorough; each step was explained with care, ensuring that evidence was meticulously collected and documented, along with her taking photographs, all while attending to my immediate medical needs. When I caught sight of my reflection in the hospital room mirror, the full impact of the assault hit me. Tears streamed down my cheeks as I fully viewed my black, blue, and purple bruised body. Despite feeling shattered and alone, this was a pivotal moment of realization — my reflection showed not just a victim but the beginning stages of a survivor confronting the reality of her situation.

This pivotal hospital visit marked the first step in acknowledging the depth of my trauma. Despite the lingering stigma within the military about seeking such help and the fear of potentially losing my security clearance, I scheduled subsequent appointments with mental health services. This added layer of anxiety underscored the complex dynamics of recovering while steering through the bureaucratic challenges that often discourage service members from seeking the mental health support they critically need.

At each duty station, you would hear about domestic violence, assault, or intimate partner violence (IPV), which in the military is alarmingly common, yet one never fully grasps the frequency of those events until it becomes personal. Statistics reveal that up to 58% of service members may experience IPV, highlighting a deeply rooted issue that cuts across individual and systemic lines. This chapter of my life began a transformative journey — stepping into silence, then seclusion, healing, reflection, and gradually empowerment. As I faced these challenges, the broader epidemic of IPV within the military framed my personal ordeal within a larger context, driving home the critical need for systemic change and support for those in similar straits.[1]

THE SILENCE THAT SCREAMS

In the solitude that followed the assault, a deep silence enveloped my world. I went from the bubbly, outgoing, outspoken Speaking about the incident felt like crossing through a minefield of memories; silence became my shield — a very heavy shield. The laughter from cartoons echoed hollowly in my apartment, a stark contrast to the turmoil within. When a friend's voice over the phone innocently yet accusingly questioned, "Are you going back to him?" I was stunned. Their words felt like an accusation, a disbelief in the severity of my pain. "No," I whispered, severing the connection with them. Their question echoed in my mind, amplifying my self-imposed isolation. I couldn't bear the thought of explaining or justifying my decision to stay away, so I chose silence.

---

[1] Spotswood, Stephen. 2022. "Intimate Partner Violence More Common with Veterans, Military Personnel." U.S. Medicine. November 9, 2022. https://www.usmedicine.com/clinical-topics/womens-health/intimate-partner-violence-more-common-with-veterans-military-personnel/.

The echo of that conversation lingered long after. My days became a routine devoid of real connection: work, then home to the false cheer of anything and all things comedy and cartoons. The judge's denial of a restraining order, citing concerns over my assailant's potential law enforcement career, felt like a secondary betrayal. The system that was supposed to protect me seemed more concerned with his future than my safety. My home, once a sanctuary, now felt like a cage filled with haunting memories and relentless questions. Why me? How could this happen? Was there a way to prevent it?

Amidst this backdrop, my cat offered the only solace — his presence a constant comfort, his silence not demanding answers I wasn't ready to give. This small creature provided a touchstone to a life before chaos; their simple acts of affection were a lifeline in the streams of my despair. My cat reminded me that reaching out and finding support was possible even when words felt like insurmountable obstacles. My choice to remain silent was my own, but so too was the decision to eventually seek help, to find a way to voice my pain in a sea of silence that seemed to swallow me each day.

As the days turned to weeks, the silence that I had clung to turned to screams. It called out the unspoken, the buried, and the denied. It challenged me to confront the shadows and to question whether the facade of normalcy was worth the price of my voice. The deafening silence held the echoes of my unresolved struggle, a loudness that awaited acknowledgement and understanding.

This chapter of my life, marked by shadows and silence, was just the beginning. As I teetered on the edge of despair and empowerment, I realized that breaking the silence was not just about speaking out — it was about screaming back at the darkness and, in doing so, reclaiming the vibrancy of a spirit too long shrouded in the aftermath of trauma.

New Horizons: Stepping Beyond the Shadows

Leaving the military was a decision shrouded in uncertainty, yet it stemmed from a profound necessity for healing — a healing distanced from the memories and faces that echoed past trauma. Over the years, the military was more than just a career; it had been my community, my identity. But as the chapters of my life turned, it became evident that my path lay beyond the structured confines of military life. Stepping away was not merely an end but a bold commencement of something new — an opportunity to rediscover my dignity, peace, and perhaps a new version of life itself.

The transition was daunting. An unsettling quiet accompanied my newfound freedom, replacing the familiarity of regimented days. This solitude, however, was not just about being alone; it was about introspection and taking the first tentative steps towards self-reclamation.

I was not alone in this journey. All across the nation, there were others like me — women who had donned uniforms with pride but found themselves at crossroads, compelled to choose paths less traveled by their peers. Our stories, varied as they were, wove together into a tapestry rich with resilience and hope. The shared experiences connected us, creating a silent sisterhood of strength found in the solitude of our individual journeys.

As I forged this new path, I embraced the unknown with cautious optimism. The decision to leave was loaded with fears and 'what-ifs,' but it was also filled with possibilities of what could be. It was a leap into uncharted waters, a surrender to the currents of life that promised new lessons, new challenges, and new joys.

This chapter of transition was not just about moving away from what was familiar, but also towards what could be. It was about transforming solitude from a state of loneliness to a state of reflective, productive peace. It marked a significant shift from enduring external battles to confronting and conquering internal ones.

As I settled into these new thoughts and new rhythm of life, the once overwhelming silence began to whisper tales of hope and renewal. The solitude transformed from a reminder of isolation to a companion in healing, gently guiding me through the process of rebuilding a life disentangled from an unwelcome and unexpected trauma.

A New Chapter in the Middle East

The decision to relocate to Qatar marked the beginning of a profound transformation in my life. It wasn't just a change of scenery; it was a leap into a rich tapestry of culture, tradition, and personal growth. The Middle East, with its unique blend of ancient traditions and modern extravagance, offered a stark contrast to my past life and a fresh canvas on which to redraw my identity.

Embracing New Surroundings

Upon my arrival in Qatar, I discovered an opulent world bursting with wealth and luxury, from towering skyscrapers to lush, sprawling shopping centers. The richness of Arabic culture was evident in every market, every meal, and the melodious calls to prayer that punctuated the day. These calls became a spiritual anchor, reminding me to pause and reflect, to give thanks, and to contemplate what I held sacred. This daily ritual became a crucial part of my healing, anchoring me to a routine that fostered spiritual growth and inner peace.

Cultural Immersion and Healing

Living in such an exotic land constantly exposed me to new experiences that pushed the boundaries of my comfort zone and challenged my perceptions. I learned to navigate the nuances of Arabic etiquette and customs, finding joy in the challenge as well as the small victories of successful interactions. The warm hospitality of the Qatari people played a significant role in this transition, as they welcomed me with open arms, eager to share their culture and traditions.

The vibrant expatriate community became a second family, a network of individuals from diverse backgrounds who shared similar stories of seeking new beginnings. Within this community, I found others who had faced their own battles with trauma and were similarly using their time abroad to heal. These connections were invaluable, providing support and understanding that transcended cultural divides.

Reflection and Growth

As I settled into my new life, the initial thrill of novelty gave way to deeper reflections on my past experiences. The physical distance from my previous life allowed me to see the events that had shaped me with new clarity. I began to understand how my experiences had impacted my trust in others and my self-worth, and with this understanding, I started to rebuild, thread by delicate thread.

The opportunity to work in such a dynamic environment also played a pivotal role in my recovery. It offered not just a distraction but a meaningful challenge that helped rebuild my confidence. The professional environment in Qatar, while demanding, was also incredibly rewarding, and it pushed me to achieve new levels of success and fulfillment.

Looking Ahead

For those considering a similar path—changing not just careers but countries — the journey offers both monumental challenges and unparalleled opportunities for growth. It is essential to seek professional help to manage the long-term effects of trauma effectively. Most countries with large expatriate communities offer invaluable resources like counseling and support groups for expatriates.

This chapter of my life, rich with new experiences and personal discovery, underscored the importance of embracing change and the potential for renewal. It taught me that sometimes, to find peace, one must take bold steps into the unknown, trusting in the journey to lead to a place of greater strength and understanding.

Focusing Forward: Mastering the Mind Post-Trauma

Living and working abroad had been a transformative experience, immersing me in new cultures and providing a sense of freedom that was both exhilarating and therapeutic. The distance and change of environment helped mask some of the deeper, lingering issues stemming from the assault I had endured years earlier. However, this displacement also inadvertently delayed confronting the underlying trauma directly, prolonging my journey toward mental recovery.

Being Diagnosed

It wasn't until 16 years after the military assault that I was formally diagnosed with PTSD. This diagnosis was a pivotal moment — it not only explained the range of emotions, nightmares, and occasional day-time flashbacks I experienced but also marked a new chapter in my approach to healing. Understanding what I was battling was the first step towards targeted recovery, allowing me to adopt specific strategies to manage and mitigate the symptoms.

My recovery path was anything but linear. It involved cycles of progress and setbacks, underscoring the non-linear nature of healing from PTSD. I engaged in various therapies, including new virtual therapy options that had become widely accessible by 2024. These digital platforms provided flexibility and privacy, reducing the stigma associated with seeking mental health support and allowing consistent care regardless of my geographic location. The importance of community — both locally and online — became more evident as I connected with others who shared similar experiences. These connections fostered a sense of belonging and understanding that was vital for my healing process.

The latest statistics on PTSD recovery highlight promising trends. Recent advancements in PTSD treatment show significant success rates among veterans, offering hope to many who struggle. For example, the introduction of prolonged exposure therapy, which did not work for me, and cognitive processing therapy have been shown to significantly reduce PTSD symptoms in veterans, with many reporting substantial improvement in their quality of life. In addition to Prolonged Exposure Therapy (PE) and Cognitive Processing Therapy (CPT), which have shown significant success in treating PTSD among veterans, there are several other treatment modalities that have been effective:

Eye Movement Desensitization and Reprocessing (EMDR): This therapy is designed to alleviate the distress associated with traumatic memories. EMDR therapy involves the veteran focusing on a traumatic memory while experiencing bilateral stimulation (typically eye movements), which is associated with a reduction in the vividness and emotion associated with the trauma memories.

Medication: Certain medications, whether natural or prescribed, such as selective serotonin reuptake inhibitors (SSRIs) and serotonin-norepinephrine reuptake inhibitors (SNRIs), have been approved by the FDA for treating PTSD. These medications can help control the symptoms of depression and anxiety, which often accompany PTSD. Be sure to seek a doctor's recommendation for your own specific treatment.

Group Therapy: Participating in group therapy allows veterans to share their experiences and coping strategies and to gain support from peers who have faced similar challenges. This can decrease feelings of isolation and help build a community of support.

Mindfulness-Based Stress Reduction (MBSR): This therapy incorporates techniques such as meditation, body awareness, and yoga to help people become more aware of the present moment and less reactive to stress. MBSR has been adapted for veterans with PTSD and has shown promise in reducing symptoms.

Narrative Exposure Therapy (NET): This treatment is particularly useful for individuals with complex and multiple traumatic events. NET involves the creation of a chronological narrative of the individual's life, focusing on traumatic experiences, which helps to contextualize and process these events.

Each of these therapies has unique methods and advantages, and it is possible to customize them to each veteran's unique PTSD needs.

Focusing Forward

As I continued to focus on my career and personal development, pursuing certifications, attending conferences, and enrolling in courses not only diverted my mind from traumatic memories but also helped me build a future that felt both purposeful and promising. Each step forward in my education and career was a step away from my past traumas, embodying the mantra of focusing forward.

This chapter of my life, while marked by challenges, is also a testament to the resilience and tenacity of the human spirit. It underscores the importance of addressing mental health head-on, utilizing available resources, and continually striving for personal growth and healing.

Rebuilding Trust and Relationships

Rebuilding trust and relationships after trauma involves a multifaceted journey through self-discovery, cautious interaction, and the slow dismantling of the walls built by past hurts. As I navigated the delicate terrains of new relationships and friendships, the shadow of my past trauma often loomed, subtly influencing interactions and expectations.

Relearning Intimacy

Starting new romantic relationships was particularly challenging. The echoes of past abuse instilled a cautious approach to intimacy and trust. I found myself setting strict boundaries, such as not revealing where I lived until at least six months into the relationship. This rule was my safety net, giving me the space and time to assess trustworthiness and compatibility without the immediate pressures of deeper commitment.

The fear of repeating past patterns also meant I was quick to pull away at signs of potential conflict or discomfort. This reaction, while protective, often confused those I dated and made it difficult to form lasting connections. Many women who experience PTSD following an assault face similar challenges — they may perceive danger where there is none or feel disproportionately vulnerable during routine disagreements, complicating their ability to maintain healthy relationships.

REBUILDING FRIENDSHIPS

Reconnecting with old friends was another critical aspect of my healing journey. Initially, I avoided discussing the assault, focusing conversations on the present and future rather than dwelling on past trauma. This approach facilitated the restoration of normalcy and prevented the constant perception of victimhood.

Over time, as my confidence in these renewed friendships grew, I gradually shared more about my past experiences. Various degrees of empathy and support met these disclosures, shaping who would become part of my closer circle. Rebuilding these friendships taught me the value of vulnerability and the strength it takes to be open about one's struggles.

SILENT BATTLES AND MOVING FORWARD

When I discussed my PTSD in the context of relationships, I discovered its hidden impacts. Many women dealing with PTSD from past assaults often suffer silently, their partners unaware of the internal battles that influence their behaviors and reactions. Recognizing this, I learned the importance of communication about one's mental health status and advocating for transparency and understanding in all my relationships.

In both dating and friendship, the emphasis shifted from seeking immediate depth to fostering gradual, organic connections. Each interaction became a step towards trusting not just the people in my life but also my judgment and instincts.

This is not only about a journey of building relationships but also reflects a deeper internal process of rebuilding trust in yourself and others. For anyone navigating similar paths, remember the importance of setting personal boundaries, the value of gradual disclosure, and the strength found in both silence and speech. This chapter of my life underscores the ongoing process of healing and the continuous effort to forge connections that are both meaningful and affirming.

Rebuilding trust and nurturing relationships post-trauma is not a linear journey but a complex interaction of self-protection, vulnerability, and gradual opening. It is about learning to balance the past with hopes for the future, understanding that each step forward is a triumph over the echoes of trauma.

Reflecting on My Journey

As I look back on the time I spent living and working across various countries in the Middle East, it's clear now that the journey was as much about running from something as it was about seeking something new. The question often posed to me, "What was I running from?" encapsulated more than just physical movement — it was a flight from unresolved feelings and past traumas that I had not fully confronted.

Living abroad, I sometimes found myself retreating into my flat from Friday evening until Monday morning, wrapped in solitude that was both comforting and isolating. These retreats were not just about physical rest but also about mental escape, providing a brief respite from the relentless pace of daily life that prevented me from facing my past.

This reflective journey highlights the importance of seeking help when grappling with deep-seated issues like depression, self-criticism, or past trauma. If I had sought professional help earlier, perhaps my path to recovery wouldn't have been as prolonged or as troubled with difficulty. The process of healing and understanding isn't something one should go through alone; reaching out for support can significantly alter the course of recovery and lead to a quicker resolution of painful emotions.

Reflecting on your journey isn't just about looking back — it's also about moving forward with the knowledge and strength gained from your experiences. You can illuminate the path for others by sharing your story, providing hope and encouraging a collective strength that fosters healing and growth. Remember, every step you take in your recovery not only reshapes your life but also casts light on the path for those who follow.

As I continue my journey of emotional recovery, I have grown increasingly adept at navigating the challenges that arise in everyday life. Each day presents opportunities to apply the lessons I've learned through therapy and self-reflection, especially in situations that once seemed daunting. Whether it's managing interactions at work, engaging with people in social settings, or handling routine tasks like shopping, I now approach these with a new level of understanding and resilience.

I've developed strategies that help mitigate stress and avoid triggers. For instance, when at work, I prioritize clear communication and set boundaries to maintain a healthy professional environment. In social interactions, I strive to remain present and authentic, which helps in forming genuine connections. Even something as mundane as shopping has become easier as I implement mindfulness techniques to stay focused and calm. With each step forward, I find myself better equipped to handle the complexities of life with a sense of confidence and a toolkit of coping mechanisms. These skills not only enhance my own well-being but also improve my interactions with others, contributing to a more fulfilling and balanced life.

DaVonda St. Clair

DaVonda St.Clair, a breast cancer survivor and Service Disabled Veteran, launched her career in Logistics within the U.S military and has since ascended to become a notable Information Security Architect, a position seldom held by women of color globally. She is the creator of the Tech Should Be Female and Beautifully me coloring book series, inspiring young Black girls in tech and self-empowerment. DaVonda holds numerous business and technology certifications, is Board Certified in Organizational Leadership, and is actively pursuing a PhD in the same discipline.

Connect with DaVonda at https://www.linkedin.com/in/davondastclair.

REFLECTION QUESTIONS

1. The delayed PTSD diagnosis years after the inciting event underscores how trauma can have long-lasting effects. How can increasing awareness about the range of post-traumatic responses help individuals identify issues and access care sooner?

REFLECTION QUESTIONS

2. The author's move to Qatar provided a fresh start and new perspectives. How might changing one's environment or surrounding oneself with different cultures impact the healing process after trauma?

_____

_____

_____

_____

_____

_____

_____

_____

_____

_____

_____

_____

_____

_____

REFLECTION QUESTIONS

3. What lessons can we learn from the author's story about resilience, focusing forward, and not letting past traumas define one's future path?

Chapter 4 | Dr. Carrie Young-McWilliams

Misread Minds
A Battle with Anxiety and Mood Adjustment Disorder

> *In the garden of life, I chose to cultivate and nourish the petals of charity, care, and compassion of the flower that is my soul, while steadfastly rejecting the harsh winds of family, friends, and career exploitation that sought to wither the tender blooms of my generosity.*
>
> —Dr. Carrie Young-McWilliams

INTRODUCTION

In the tapestry of life, each thread represents a story, a struggle, or a triumph that contributes to the intricate patterns of our existence. My name is Carrie Young-McWilliams, and the narrative I wish to share unfolds across the landscapes of Mississippi and beyond, weaving through the realms of personal challenges, professional hurdles, and the silent battles fought within the confines of the mind. Mental health, a cornerstone of our well-being, often remains shrouded in silence, especially within marginalized communities where the echo of unspoken pain reverberates through generations.

Raised in an environment where discussions of mental health were as rare as a cool breeze on a sweltering summer day, I navigated the complexities of life feeling misunderstood and out of place. Nevertheless, I came to see myself as a tall, statuesque Black Queen grappling with the invisible foes of anxiety, depression, and an adjustment disorder that went unnamed for too long. My journey from a child yearning for acceptance in Mississippi to an advocate for mental health in the educational system is a testament to resilience, the power of self-awareness, and the unyielding support of the strong Black Southern women who raised me.

This narrative is not just mine; it reflects the silent struggles of many and serves as a beacon of hope and a call to action. By sharing my story, I aim to illuminate the path for others, advocating for a world where mental health is not an afterthought but a central aspect of our collective well-being. Join me on this journey through the valleys of despair and the peaks of triumph as we explore the essence of resilience, understanding, and the transformative power of speaking out.

Childhood in Mississippi: The Silent Echoes of Mental Health

I began my journey in the heart of Mississippi, where the roots of family trees run deep, and the air is thick with unspoken histories. Here, amidst the rich tapestry of Southern life, mental health remained a ghostly presence, acknowledged only in hushed tones and euphemisms. A profound sense of disconnection marked my childhood, split between the nurturing environments of my grandparents' homes and our community's vibrant, sometimes chaotic life. This dissonance wasn't just about feeling physically distinct as a tall, young Black girl in a world that seemed to predefine my place. It was a silent battle with feelings of anxiety and depression — a struggle for understanding in a culture where such discussions were as scarce as rain in a drought.

Navigating Social Challenges: Alienation and the Quest for Acceptance

Growing up, my social circle was a close-knit fabric of family, friends, and church members. Yet, despite the physical closeness, an invisible chasm lay between me and true belonging. My peers often branded me as socially awkward, a label that stung with every misunderstanding and misplaced joke. Their words, though perhaps unintended in their cruelty, echoed the broader societal stigma surrounding mental health. It wasn't just my stature that set me apart; it was my internal world — a realm of constant analysis where every interaction was dissected to find a way to fit in.

The tumultuous seas of adolescence amplified the alienation I felt. My quest for acceptance found a dangerous harbor in relationships, particularly with boys whose attention seemed, at the time, to offer a balm for my isolation. Yet this search for belonging led me into the stormy waters of a toxic relationship. For four years, I weathered the cycles of verbal and physical abuse, a reflection of the internalized fear of rejection that had shadowed me from a young age.

THE INFLUENCE OF STRONG BLACK SOUTHERN WOMEN

In the midst of these trials, the unwavering strength of the Black Southern women who raised me offered a beacon of hope. These matriarchs, who navigated the complexities of life with grace and resilience, instilled in me the values of direct communication and self-assurance. From them, I learned the power of my voice and the importance of articulating my desires and thoughts without reservation. Yet, even as I began to embrace these lessons, my attempts to assert myself often met with misunderstanding. My directness, a trait honed by the examples of these formidable women, sometimes clashed with the expectations of others, leaving me stranded on the island of misinterpretation once more.

Lessons Learned and Paths Forward

As I navigated the journey from childhood into young adulthood, my challenges served as harsh but invaluable teachers. The alienation and misunderstanding, the painful years spent in a toxic relationship, and the struggle to find my voice amidst the cacophony of societal expectations taught me about the complexity of human interaction and the importance of authentic self-expression. These experiences paved the way for my subsequent advocacy for mental health awareness and support, especially in historically marginalized communities that greatly require these conversations.

Through reflection and growth, I came to understand that my feelings of disconnection and my battles with anxiety and depression were not signs of weakness but indicators of a deeper need for understanding and support. This realization marked the beginning of my journey toward healing and advocacy. This path would lead me to confront and challenge the stigmas surrounding mental health in both my personal and professional lives.

Embarking on a Path of Education and Advocacy

The matriarchs in my life laid a solid foundation, inspiring me to venture into the world of education with a vision to make a difference. A burning desire to positively influence young minds marked the transition from my personal struggles to the professional arena. This aspiration was not merely a career choice, but a calling driven by my experiences and the lessons learned from the strong, resilient women who shaped me, spoke to my potential, and never gave up on me.

The Joy of Impact and the Shadow of Misunderstanding

The initial years of my career were a testament to the transformative power of education. Witnessing the growth and development of my students filled me with an unparalleled sense of fulfillment. However, as much as I thrived in impacting young lives, I encountered barriers that seemed all too familiar — misunderstandings and misinterpretations of my actions and demeanor by colleagues.

The feedback I received in my first role in educational administration was a jarring echo of my past. Colleagues perceived my demeanor as intimidating, a label that left me perplexed and introspective. My intentions were always to uplift and support, never to dominate or intimidate. This period of self-reflection served as a painful reminder of the challenges I encountered growing up, where my upbringing often misinterpreted my assertiveness as aggression.

Navigating Misinterpretations: The Struggle for Understanding

One particularly painful misunderstanding involved my involuntary physical reactions, often misinterpreted as signs of aggression. Anxiety-induced constriction interpreted my high-pitched voice as yelling. My rapid speech, meant to convey thoughts efficiently, was seen as an unwillingness to listen. These misinterpretations were not just personal affronts, but professional obstacles that hindered my ability to connect with colleagues and foster, from the perspective of the cultural majority, a collaborative environment.

As I advanced in my career, the feedback pattern highlighting my supposedly intimidating nature persisted. This repetitive critique forced me to confront a crucial realization: the need to bridge the gap between my intentions and others' perceptions. It was a daunting task that required me to reassess and adapt my communication style while maintaining the essence of who I am.

The Journey Toward Self-Reflection and Effective Communication

This period of introspection and adjustment was challenging yet transformative. It taught me the importance of clear, empathetic communication, as well as the need to understand the perspectives of those around me. As I refined my approach, I became acutely aware of the systemic barriers that often silence Black female voices in professional settings. My experiences underscored the critical need for diversity, equity, and inclusion initiatives that not only acknowledge but actively address the unique challenges faced by Black female educators.

Moments of Crisis: Confronting Health and Systemic Challenges

The path to self-awareness and professional growth was not smooth. Amid the triumphs and challenges of my career, a crisis loomed—a crisis of health and well-being that threatened to derail everything I had worked towards.

A Stark Revelation: The Toll of Neglect

A routine visit to my doctor unveiled a harsh reality: the years of prioritizing others' needs over my own had taken a severe toll on my health. The diagnosis was a litany of concerns—severe dehydration, elevated blood pressure, and signs of systemic failure—all symptoms of the relentless stress and anxiety I had endured. This moment was a wake-up call, a stark realization that I could no longer ignore the needs of my body and mind.

Hospitalization: A Call to Prioritize Self-Care

The days I spent in the hospital were a period of forced reflection. Separated from the hustle of professional life, I confronted the unsustainable nature of my work-life balance. My family's support and concern, coupled with the stark environment of the hospital room, crystallized the need for a change. I recognized that true strength lies not in relentless perseverance but in the courage to prioritize one's health and well-being.

The Decision to Step Back: Choosing Health Over Career

Leaving my position was a difficult decision, fraught with fear and uncertainty. Yet, it was a necessary step toward healing. The subsequent years, filled with similar challenges in different settings, underscored the systemic nature of the issues I faced. The cycle of stress, anxiety, and health problems persisted until I made a radical change—seeking a role that minimized direct interaction and offered a semblance of the balance I desperately needed.

Seeking and Creating Change: A New Professional Chapter

The transition to a consulting role was a breath of fresh air. It allowed me to engage with the educational community on my terms, focusing on the quality and impact of my work without the daily stresses of administration. This career period was transformative, offering a glimpse of the dream job I had envisioned. Landing my dream job initially felt like a triumph, a long-awaited acknowledgment of my hard work and aspirations. It promised an opportunity to utilize my skills in an environment that supported and nurtured my professional growth. However, the reality of this dream job quickly unraveled into a facade. When I mustered the courage to advocate for myself and articulate the accommodations and support, I needed to thrive and contribute my best work, my voice was met with disdain.

Jokes dismissed my requests for understanding, harassment met my earnest efforts to foster positive change, and discrimination countered my pleas for equity. What was once a beacon of hope and achievement transformed into a nightmare, a stark reminder of the chasm between the ideal of an inclusive, supportive workplace and the harsh reality of systemic indifference and bias that still pervades even the most progressive of spaces. This experience, though disheartening, ignited a deeper resolve within me to fight for a future where no one has to endure such disillusionment in their pursuit of professional fulfillment.

The Impact of COVID-19: Challenges and Opportunities

The onset of the COVID-19 pandemic introduced new challenges but also unexpected opportunities. The shift to remote work, while isolating, alleviated some of the anxiety associated with direct interactions. However, the retirement of a key organizational leader and the subsequent shift in dynamics revealed the fragile nature of my newfound balance.

Confrontations and Advocacy for Mental Health Accommodations

A confrontation during a virtual meeting, stemming from my anxiety-driven preference to avoid on-camera interactions, highlighted the ongoing struggle for mental health recognition in the workplace. Despite seeking accommodations, the response from my organization was disheartening — placing me on administrative leave and ultimately denying my request for necessary adjustments.

This experience illuminated the broader issue of mental health support in professional settings, especially for Black female educators. The denial of accommodations, as well as the lack of understanding and support, highlighted the urgent need for systemic change. It was a painful yet enlightening chapter, reinforcing my commitment to advocacy and pursuing a healthier, more supportive work environment.

Navigating the Personal Impact of Mental Health Challenges

My personal relationships, particularly my marriage, mirrored and magnified the toll of my professional life on my mental health. After thirty-one years with my college sweetheart, the man who had been my rock and partner through myriad life changes, I faced one of the most heartbreaking decisions of my life: to leave. This decision wasn't made lightly; it was the culmination of years of struggling to balance my mental health needs with our lives together.

The Decision to Leave: A Crossroads of Love and Self-Preservation

Our relationship, while filled with love and shared history, became unsustainable as my mental health issues deepened. Despite his unwavering support, there was a fundamental disconnect in my understanding of the impact of my struggles with anxiety, depression, and mood swings. I realized that to truly heal and manage my condition, I needed a space where I could prioritize my well-being without the added stress of navigating our complex dynamic. This realization led me to make the difficult choice to leave, not out of a lack of love but as an act of self-preservation.

Embracing Change: The Journey Toward Healing and Independence

Leaving my marriage was a pivotal step on my journey towards self-discovery and healing. It marked the beginning of a new chapter where I could focus entirely on my mental health and well-being. As selfish as it may sound, I needed it. This period of solitude and reflection was instrumental in understanding my needs, limitations, and the importance of creating an environment conducive to healing. It was a time of profound growth, where I learned the value of self-care, setting boundaries, and having the courage to make difficult choices for my health.

Fostering Advocacy Through Personal Experience

My journey through personal struggles and professional challenges has been a powerful catalyst for my advocacy work. By sharing my story, I aim to illuminate the path for others facing similar battles, advocating for systemic changes that support mental health awareness and accommodations in the workplace, especially for Black female educators. No longer will I share my vulnerabilities in white spaces for their benefit, but for the benefit of people who look like me and my children to heal and learn how to care for themselves. My story comes at a cost; I will no longer sell out so that the cultural majority can engage in performative actions.

ENGAGING WITH COMMUNITIES: A MISSION TO SUPPORT AND EDUCATE

My commitment to advocacy extends beyond the professional sphere; it's about engaging with parents, students, and communities to foster understanding and support for mental health. Through workshops, speaking engagements, and personal interactions, I strive to demystify mental health issues, sharing my narrative to reassure others that they are not alone in their struggles. This work is not just about awareness; it's about building a support network that empowers individuals to advocate for their needs and well-being.

ADVOCACY GOALS: CALLING FOR SYSTEMIC CHANGE

As I look forward, my advocacy focuses on several key areas:

<u>Promoting Diversity, Equity, and Inclusion</u>: By working with educational institutions to prioritize DEI initiatives, I aim to create environments that respect and value the experiences of Black female educators, mitigating feelings of isolation and marginalization.

<u>Acknowledging and Rewarding Contributions</u>: It's crucial to ensure that Black female educators receive the credit they deserve for their work, recognizing their intellectual property and contributions without relegating them to a checkbox on a diversity quota.

<u>Establishing Mental Health Support Systems</u>: Collaborating with schools and boards to develop targeted mental health resources and services that address the unique challenges faced by educators, ensuring these systems are accessible and effective.

<u>Advocating for Work-Life Balance</u>: Promoting policies that support a healthy work-life balance, recognizing the demanding nature of the educational profession, and providing resources for stress management and self-care.

CONCLUSION

Creating a supportive environment for Black female educators like me involves more than just awareness; it requires actionable change. By prioritizing diversity, equity, and inclusion, acknowledging our contributions, establishing robust mental health support systems, and promoting work-life balance, educational institutions can begin to address the systemic challenges that impact our well-being.

My journey from a young girl in Mississippi to an advocate for mental health and education has been fraught with challenges. Still, it has also been a growth, discovery, and empowerment journey. By sharing my story, I inspire others to recognize their worth, advocate for their needs, and support one another in the journey toward healing and fulfillment.

Through advocacy, engagement, and a relentless pursuit of systemic change, we can create a future where mental health is prioritized, support systems are effective and accessible, and Black female educators feel valued, understood, and empowered to thrive in their personal and professional lives. This is not just my mission; it's a call to action for all of us to build a more compassionate, inclusive, and supportive society for generations to come.

DR. CARRIE YOUNG-MCWILLIAMS

Dr. Carrie Young-McWilliams: a dynamic force whose journey has spanned roles as a dedicated educator, a supportive Navy wife, and now, the visionary CEO of Young-McWilliams Consulting, LLC. With her passion for fostering growth and empowerment, she co-founded EmpowerED Solutions by Young & Horner, LLC. Driven by her deep commitment to educational excellence, she pursued and achieved a Doctorate in Educational Leadership. But Carrie's talents don't stop there; she's also a creative soul, expressing herself as a blogger, poet, and captivating keynote speaker. Her workshops and coaching sessions testify to her versatility, offering insights as a trainer, mentor, curriculum writer, and presenter.

What truly sets Carrie apart is her unwavering advocacy for social justice and her unique ability to connect with people across a spectrum, from young minds in their formative years to those in the later stages of life. Her approach? A perfect blend of humor and gravitas. She draws you in with laughter, and with her compelling messages, she leaves a lasting impact. Her work as a National Equity Project Fellow speaks volumes about her commitment to equity, and her peers have celebrated her as a trailblazer in digital literacy.

Carrie's multifaceted career is not just about achievements and accolades; it reflects her genuine passion for making a difference in the world. Dr. Young-McWilliams is a beacon of inspiration, guiding those around her toward a brighter, more equitable future through the spoken word, a written line, or a strategic initiative.

REFLECTION QUESTIONS

1. How does the author's journey challenge and expand your understanding of the impact of mental health on personal and professional life, especially within historically marginalized communities?

REFLECTION QUESTIONS

2. Reflect on the role of systemic barriers in exacerbating mental health issues for female educators. How can institutions implement inclusive and supportive policies based on the author's experiences and suggestions?

REFLECTION QUESTIONS

3. Throughout her journey, the author faced misunderstandings, lack of support, and denial of accommodations related to her mental health in professional settings. How can workplaces improve in providing appropriate accommodations for women and marginalized groups?

Chapter 5 | Shakira Releford

What We Know About OCD is Dead Wrong

Owning our story can be hard but not nearly as difficult as spending our lives running from it.

—Dr. Brené Brown

Growing up in the late 80s and early 90s wasn't that different from today. Systemic racism and social injustices still affect Black and Latino families in urban communities. There was still police brutality against minority groups, specifically Black men. I can remember turning on the TV and hearing the news about Rodney King and the looting and protests that took place on his behalf. That was very similar to what transpired after the George Floyd incident in 2020.

In the 1990s, there was so much publicity and media coverage around the O.J. Simpson trial and the Menendez brothers. Besides that, political scandals took place, specifically with President Bill Clinton and Monica Lewinsky.

Family meant everything to Black and Latino families. Families intentionally got together, for any reason, to celebrate all life events. Whether it was a Saturday morning funeral or Aunt Beatrice's 4th of July cookout, the gathering of family provided a sense of safety, security, and even a sense of belonging. The connection to family and cultural origins helped Blacks and Latinos develop a stronger sense of self, social constructs, and mental frameworks. It gave us more freedom and liberty to explore self-expression.

I was born and raised in the urban city of East Chicago, Indiana (EC). EC is in the middle of two major cities, Gary and Hammond, Indiana. Being white in my neighborhood meant being in the minority because EC is predominantly made up of working-class Black and Latino Americans. Whether Catholic, Jehovah's Witness, or any other Christian faith (including COGIC, Baptist, or Pentecostal), most city residents belonged to a religious group, signifying their connection to a higher power. Their faith allowed them to persevere amid adversity.

My mother, her siblings, her parents, and nieces and nephews all lived between EC, Gary, and Hammond, which meant that my family was very close. I could develop my self-identity, mental framework, and self-expression, except for this one thing: my OCD.

I remember being as young as five years old and experiencing the O-C cycle. I learned very early on that all the misconceptions about obsessive-compulsive disorder (OCD) were, in fact, the only symptoms of the disorder. My mom would say I had OCD, but I would say, "Oh, I'm not a germophobe," or "I'm not that much of a neat freak," so I didn't think anything of it. Little did I know I was the little black poster child for OCD, because the origins of my obsessions are what led to my compulsive behaviors as I grew up.

As a child, I had to have everything symmetrically "just right.". All of my clothes in my closet were one-and-a-half inches apart, and I was constantly shifting them over and over and over until they "felt right.". I would turn knobs and flick light switches a certain number of times, obsessing about whether I was a "good friend" to my peers and what they thought of me, constantly ripping up the paper every time I didn't write a word "a certain way," collecting and saving all of my schoolwork in a particular drawer because I would have anxiety about what would happen if I didn't reflect on all of my good achievements, and excessive cleaning, to name a few.

Once I reached middle school, these compulsive behaviors became more noticeable to my family and friends. People began to tease me frequently and refer to me as "weird." My mom always told me that she thought I had OCD because of my excessive hair-pulling. I was unaware of the direct correlation between trichotillomania, or excessive hair pulling, and OCD.

Because I didn't have many friends, I believed what people told me about being weird. I let a lot of my intrusive thoughts hinder my relationships with my peers because I had anxiety about whether I was a good friend to them or if they liked me. This anxiety spiraled into compulsive picking at the stitching on all my T-shirts and pulling my hair out of style. My compulsions gave me so much relief from the anxiety, yet I felt that every time I would have an obsession or intrusive thought, I believed I was just going to hell for having these thoughts, so I would engage in the compulsions again.

As I got older, the O-C cycle worsened. The self-identity, self-compassion, and self-expression I once possessed had become nonexistent by the time I started college in 2008.

In 2008, I was a student at Indiana University-Bloomington (IUB). I had just graduated high school, and going straight to college during that summer was an adventure. College is like the hit TV show theme song "A Different World," because you have many people from many walks of life all in one place and having to process everyone else's lived experiences was exciting yet overstimulating at the same time.

I feel proud to be a first-generation college student, yet I felt that I had to keep my OCD a big secret from people. I was convinced that if people got to know the real me, they would run. I met all of my best friends through the GROUPS Scholarship Program. To this day, we are still great friends, but they had to endure a lot of my O-C cycles. None of them understood what was going on with me, but they supported me better than I deserved. With the demands of college, working two jobs, and O-C cycles, I began to have a mental breakdown.

I took advantage of the university's mental health clinic. A mental health professional on campus provided two free sessions for each student. I was excited about getting help because I had not yet received an official diagnosis.

The white graduate student I met with was completing her psychology clinical hours, and she confirmed for me that I had trichotillomania. She could not explain much else that was going on with me (my O-C cycles); other than that, it could just be "stress from being in college." This young, white woman made it apparent to me that Black people struggle more than white people do in college, so that could be why I'm having such a hard time. I wasn't heard. I didn't understand. I didn't feel valued.

As I grew older, the O-C cycle became my primary coping mechanism because intrusive thoughts became more volatile. It was hard for me to not engage in my compulsive behaviors because if I didn't, that would mean that my obsessions were valid. I felt I had to protect myself and others, which was how I could justify those compulsive behaviors. I just classified them as "quirks."

I was 24 years old and on the verge of marriage. My fiancé (now husband) was aware of my O-C cycles, but I still didn't have a diagnosis. I began going to Celebrate Recovery, a Christ-centered support and recovery group. I knew I needed help, and I loved Celebrate Recovery because it was the best help I could've received during that time of my life. My O-C cycles reduced drastically, I learned effective self-regulation skills, and I had a sponsor and people who "surrounded me" even though they all had their hurts, habits, and hang-ups. I knew Jesus had healed me, and I could gain confidence and clarity about myself.

In 2022, I received my official diagnosis of OCD. My life up to that point had been a roller coaster of highs and lows, but I don't regret them.

After working in the social work and public health sectors, I decided to advance my skills to support and advocate for others like me. One of the greatest takeaways I learned in my Positive Intelligence Coaching Program is that I can see how OCD has become more of a gift than a hindrance, which differs from how I felt about it when I was younger.

Through the work of Celebrate Recovery, Positive Intelligence, and my professional work experience, I learned how to manage my obsessive thoughts and compulsive behaviors. I developed my sage powers so I can lead with empathy, allow myself to live a life of self-compassion, and teach others to do the same (young and old alike). That doesn't mean that my O-C cycles are nonexistent, but it means that I know who I am and the exact measures I need to take to remain in control of my life and not let my OCD control me.

Understanding the intricate landscape of OCD requires peeling back layers of common misconceptions and shining a light on the reality beneath. Exploring OCD takes us beyond clinical definitions, uncovering the authentic experiences of people like me and shedding light on this misunderstood condition.

Diving deep, we must first navigate the essential terminology that forms the backbone of our understanding. At the heart of our exploration are terms such as "obsessive-compulsive disorder," "obsessions," "compulsions," "rituals," and "anxiety." Each word guides us through the fog of generalizations to the clarity of comprehension.

WHAT IS OCD?

Obsessive-Compulsive Disorder is a psychiatric diagnosis characterized by unwanted thoughts and behaviors that a person feels compelled to perform.[1] OCD often lurks in the shadows of society, its true nature obscured by misconceptions and stigma. Behind closed doors, people with OCD face a relentless emotional rollercoaster, battling intrusive thoughts and compulsions that disrupt their daily lives.

In their private lives, people with OCD struggle with intrusive thoughts and compulsive behaviors that cause disruptions to their lives. Other OCD-related tendencies that shadow closely behind OCD include anxiety, hoarding (collecting things), trichotillomania (hair pulling), and excoriation (skin picking). They act as compulsive "agents" for the emotional response to the anticipation of future threats or distress triggered by intrusive

---

[1] Quinlan, Kimberley, and Jon Hershfield. The self-compassion workbook for OCD: Lean into your fear, manage difficult emotions, & focus on recovery. Oakland, CA: New Harbinger Publication, Inc., 2021.

thoughts. These obsessions often play a significant role in both the development and maintenance of OCD.

The intensity of thoughts and behaviors, the time they consume, and the significant distress or impairment they cause in daily life distinguish OCD from everyday quirks or habits. While many of us might double-check the stove before leaving the house, people with OCD might feel compelled to check it dozens of times, the fear of causing a fire imprisoning them in a loop of checking and rechecking long past the point of reason.

At its core, OCD is like a thief that robs people of time, peace, and, occasionally, their sense of self. It is an uninvited guest at the table, dictating the terms of a person's life with an iron grip. Understanding OCD, then, is not just about recognizing the clinical symptoms but also acknowledging the profound impact on a person's life. It's about seeing beyond the rituals of the person fighting to regain control of their mind.

OCD has a spectrum of subtypes that help researchers and mental health professionals identify each category into groups for research purposes and create effective treatment plans. Here is a comprehensive list of the common subtypes of specific obsessions and compulsions.

Before I dive into the science-based tools to help you manage your OCD symptoms and even how those science-based tools and therapies worked for me, I want to briefly explain the O-C cycle. If your first encounter with OCD resembles mine, you likely encountered your initial obsession and compulsive behavior through a loop known as the O-C cycle.

Your first obsession probably presented itself in the form of a repetitive, intrusive, and possibly unwanted thought, image, feeling, sensation, or urge. Your obsessions may initially manifest as "what if" thoughts, and later, a sensation, feeling, or urge may arise in your gut, prompting you to perform an action that may have been of concern to you.

The O-C cycle goes like this: first, the obsessions begin, and then the anxiety surrounding those obsessions starts to form. Next, you engage in repetitive behavioral patterns called compulsions in hopes that they will provide a sense of relief from the anxiety. And the cycle continues.[1]

THE EMOTIONAL ROLLERCOASTER

Living with OCD is akin to riding an emotional rollercoaster with no clear end in sight. Every day presents new challenges as intrusive thoughts flood the mind, triggering overwhelming anxiety. These thoughts, often irrational and distressing, compel individuals to engage in compulsive behaviors in a futile attempt to alleviate their anxiety. The cycle repeats, trapping them in a constant state of turmoil.

At the core of OCD lies a profound sense of fear — fear of uncertainty, fear of losing control, fear of the consequences of not performing rituals. These fears can manifest in various forms, from obsessions about contamination to fears of harming oneself or others. A unique set of compulsions and rituals accompany each obsession, aimed at neutralizing the anxiety and quieting the mind.

However, compulsions only provide temporary relief, leading to a deepening sense of shame and guilt. Individuals with OCD often recognize the irrationality of their thoughts and behaviors, yet feel powerless to break

---

[1] Quinlan, Kimberley, and Jon Hershfield. The self-compassion workbook for OCD: Lean into your fear, manage difficult emotions, & focus on recovery. Oakland, CA: New Harbinger Publication, Inc., 2021.

free from their grip. This internal conflict only exacerbates their distress, fueling a cycle of self-loathing and despair.

THE STIGMA OF OCD

Beyond the internal struggles, individuals with OCD also grapple with external stigma and misunderstanding. Popular culture frequently misrepresents OCD, reduces it to stereotypes, or trivializes it for entertainment. Such portrayals not only distort the reality of the disorder but also perpetuate harmful stereotypes, further isolating those affected.

Moreover, misconceptions surrounding OCD can lead to dismissive attitudes or skepticism from others. Comments like "Just relax" or "Why don't you just stop?" undermine the severity of the disorder and invalidate the experiences of those living with it. This lack of understanding can exacerbate feelings of shame and alienation, discouraging individuals from seeking help or opening up about their struggles.

Individuals with OCD bear an even greater burden due to the widespread stigma surrounding mental illness. Fear of judgment or discrimination may prevent them from disclosing their condition to friends, family, or employers, further isolating them from much-needed support systems. As a result, many suffer in silence, hiding their struggles behind a façade of normalcy.

THE STIGMA OF OCD IN BLACK AMERICANS

The stigma associated with OCD among Black people is a complex and often overlooked aspect of mental health. While OCD can affect people of any race or ethnicity, cultural factors and societal perceptions can significantly influence Black people's experiences with the disorder.

One of the biggest obstacles for Black people with OCD is the widespread stigma surrounding mental health. Systemic racism, socioeconomic inequality, and a long-standing suspicion of the medical establishment are just a few historical and cultural elements that have fueled the stigma associated with mental illness.

Many Black communities often view mental health issues as personal weaknesses or moral failings, rather than legitimate medical conditions. This attitude can lead to reluctance or hesitation to seek help for OCD symptoms, as individuals may fear judgment or ostracism from their peers and loved ones.[1] Consequently, other coping mechanisms may mask or leave OCD symptoms untreated, resulting in prolonged suffering and a decreased quality of life.

Moreover, the intersection of race and mental health stigma can result in unique challenges for Black individuals with OCD. Cultural stereotypes and misconceptions may lead to misdiagnosis or underdiagnosis of OCD symptoms, particularly among Black youth. For instance, people may misinterpret OCD symptoms like hoarding or contamination fears as behavioral issues or cultural quirks instead of recognizing them as signs of a psychiatric disorder.

Cultural norms and attitudes can also perpetuate the stigma surrounding mental illness in the Black community. Traditional beliefs about mental health, such as the notion that seeking therapy is a sign of weakness or

---

[1] "African Americans with Obsessive Compulsive Disorder: Black Lives Matter." International OCD Foundation, August 17, 2018. https://iocdf.org/expert-opinions/african-americans-with-obsessive-compulsive-disorder-black-lives-matter/.

that prayer alone can address psychological distress, may deter individuals from seeking evidence-based treatment for OCD.

From my perspective, my family didn't address OCD, especially not as a mental health crisis. The compulsive behaviors I observed in other relatives were either "coping skills" or simply innate behaviors that everyone possesses. I believed in that framework too. I believed that the folks in my family had quirky behaviors because it was something they were born with, even though I always felt like an oddball. Once my mom shared her story with me about the trauma she experienced with my dad, I discovered the pathological pattern that existed in my family. There is a generational history of physical and emotional abuse, as well as alcoholism. Unfortunately, my dad adopted the same negative behaviors and character traits as his father, and the consequences of those patterns created a trauma response within me. The habitual exposure to the abuse during my formative years caused me to develop an insecure attachment to my dad. The O-C cycle developed out of a need for safety.

Despite their own experiences with this dysfunctional cycle, my family was unable to provide me with the understanding I sought, as they withheld much of the trauma from me for their own protection. Collectively, my grandmother, aunts, and uncles made sure I knew who my dad was but did not help me make the correlation of this generational curse out of fear I would resent him.

I struggled to convey these origins to mental health professionals. My former therapist in college often expressed sympathy and pity. She continued to receive supervision as part of her graduate program. We met twice because the university provided two free sessions per student. With each session, I did not feel safe, supported, or validated. Every time I shared with her what I was feeling, she would make me feel as though I was crazy. Throughout our sessions, her body language was filled with tension, her face twisted in a grimace, and she consistently leaned away, clearly expressing her discomfort. She struggled to empathize and be relatable to me. Because of that, I just shut down.

Ten years later, when I was 32, I found a therapist who understood me and was relatable. She had OCD too, and she could recognize and assist me in identifying my triggers for the O-C cycle. I felt secure and safe with her. Throughout our sessions, I learned how to lead with empathy in my interactions with others and myself. The way I spoke to myself was how I projected those expectations onto others, which explained to me how I sabotaged my important relationships during my early to mid-20s.

Mental health professionals must undergo cultural competency training to better understand the unique experiences and perspectives of Black individuals with OCD. Additionally, community-based initiatives, peer support groups, and culturally tailored interventions can provide a safe and supportive environment for Black individuals to seek help and share their experiences.

By destigmatizing mental illness and promoting culturally competent care, we can empower Black individuals with OCD to seek the support and treatment they need to manage their symptoms and lead fulfilling lives. Ultimately, addressing the racial stigma of OCD is essential for promoting mental health equity and ensuring that all individuals, regardless of race or ethnicity, have access to high-quality care and support.

SAGE POWERS AS A SOLUTION TO RECOVERY

In the journey of overcoming OCD, there's a profound shift that occurs when we begin to see our diagnosis not as a curse but as a gift. At first, the radical notion of viewing our diagnosis as a gift may seem counterintuitive, particularly when we find ourselves engulfed in the turmoil of intrusive thoughts and compulsive behaviors. However, emerging scientific research, particularly in positive psychology and positive intelligence, sheds light on the transformative power of this perspective.

Positive Intelligence, as conceptualized by Shirzad Chamine, introduces the notion of "sage" powers — mental capacities that enable us to navigate life with clarity, resilience, and inner peace. All of us possess inherent sage powers such as empathy, exploration, and innovation, ready for cultivation and harnessing.

In 2023, I decided to take my consulting and coaching to the next level. A few years ago, I went through a major transition from providing in-home and clinical therapy with families to education advocacy and nonprofit consultancy. The leaders I worked with were mostly neurodivergent and needed support in eliminating their intrusive and ruminating patterns of behavior and mental processes that were hindering their personal and professional growth. I did great with helping them achieve the professional growth they were looking for, but they still lacked confidence. I wanted to help my clients reach their maximum potential, as well as 10x their return on investment (ROI). I was starting to question whether I was able to be an effective consultant. One day, I stumbled upon an ad on LinkedIn about a coaching program that blends neuroscience and spirituality. In my mind, I knew I had to join this program, no matter the cost. I submitted my application and received acceptance as a grant recipient. I felt as though I was making the connection to my calling.

During my time in the Positive Intelligence Coaching Program, I began to fully understand Shizard's philosophy as it relates to the Sage Powers and OCD. I discovered that my OCD diagnosis is a gift, but it does not diminish the profound impact it has on my life or the lives of others. Rather, it reframes my perspective, empowering me to embrace my struggles as opportunities for growth and transformation. By tapping into my Sage powers of empathy, exploration, innovation, and resilience, I can transcend the limitations imposed by OCD and embark on a journey of self-discovery and fulfillment. This stuck with me because I learned how to articulate the sage powers that make sense to people like me with OCD. This framework supports me as a leader, consultant, coach, professor, and mental health advocate. My sage powers set me apart because I can incorporate this philosophy into my own practice.

In essence, the journey from seeing OCD as a curse to viewing it as a gift is a testament to the transformative power of mindset. It's a shift from victimhood to empowerment, from despair to hope, from isolation to connection. And in embracing this shift, we unlock the boundless potential that resides within each of us, OCD notwithstanding.

Positive intelligence sees OCD as a catalyst for developing and refining these sage powers. For instance, consider empathy. Those who have experienced the relentless grip of OCD firsthand are often keenly attuned to the suffering of others. This heightened sensitivity stems from a deep understanding of the pain and isolation that accompany mental illness, fostering a profound sense of empathy and compassion.

Furthermore, OCD compels us to explore the depths of our minds with unparalleled intensity. We become keen observers of our thoughts and emotions, meticulously analyzing every nuance and pattern. This introspective journey, while fraught with challenges, ultimately leads to a deeper understanding of ourselves and the human condition at large.

Innovation, another Sage power, emerges from the necessity of finding creative solutions to cope with the challenges posed by OCD. Whether it's devising new strategies to manage intrusive thoughts or experimenting with mindfulness techniques to cultivate inner peace, individuals with OCD demonstrate remarkable ingenuity and resourcefulness in navigating their condition.

Furthermore, overcoming OCD cultivates resilience, which serves as a source of strength and wisdom. Adversity, as the saying goes, is the crucible of character. In overcoming the obstacles presented by OCD, individuals develop a resilience that equips them to face life's challenges with courage and resilience.

SELF-COMPASSION AND EMPATHY AS A SOLUTION TO RECOVERY

Faced with such challenges, self-compassion and empathy emerge as powerful antidotes for those living with OCD. Self-compassion involves treating oneself with kindness, understanding, and acknowledging one's struggles without judgment or criticism. For people with OCD, cultivating self-compassion means recognizing that their thoughts and behaviors do not reflect their worth.

Similarly, empathy plays a crucial role in fostering understanding and connection. By empathizing with others who share their struggles, individuals with OCD can break free from feelings of isolation and shame. Sharing experiences with fellow sufferers can provide validation and support, affirming that they are not alone in their journey. I personally utilize this notion daily with my students. I ensure that I lead and teach with empathy first. This helps to strengthen my interpersonal communication skills and ensures I'm maintaining a learning environment of psychological safety and cultural competence.

Therapeutic approaches that emphasize self-compassion and empathy have shown promising results in the treatment of OCD. Mindfulness-based interventions, for example, encourage individuals to approach their thoughts and feelings with curiosity and acceptance rather than avoidance or judgment. Through practices such as mindfulness meditation, I have learned to observe my thoughts without becoming entangled in them, cultivating a sense of inner peace and resilience. I have reduced my O-C cycles because I have practical tools in place to help me succeed and not dwell on my perceived failures.

CONCLUSION

Obsessive-Compulsive Disorder is a complex and debilitating condition that exacts a heavy toll on those affected. Yet, beneath the surface of obsessions and compulsions lies a profound humanity — a resilience and strength that defy the stigma and misconceptions surrounding the disorder. By embracing self-compassion and empathy, I can navigate the hidden struggles of my condition with courage and compassion, paving the way for recovery and healing for myself and advocating this journey for others. Understanding and acceptance have lifted the veil of stigma, revealing the inherent dignity and worth I possess.

SHAKIRA RELEFORD

Shakira Releford is an associate professor in social and behavioral sciences. Her expertise comes from 12 years of experience as a behavior analyst, mental health professional in recovery, trauma-informed specialist, and educator. Her personal experience with OCD has motivated her to take control of her life and share her lived experience as an entrepreneur, facilitator, and trauma-informed yoga teacher to inspire others to reduce their anxiety and fulfill their purpose-driven lives. Shakira founded the 501(c)(3) nonprofit Connecting Youth Achievement Center to provide social-emotional and educational support to Black and Indigenous youth with neurodivergence in marginalized communities. Shakira uses positive intelligence and biblical teachings to help change people's lives. She works as a consultant for neurodivergent business owners and charitable organizations.

https://www.linkedin.com/in/shakira-releford

REFLECTION QUESTIONS

1. The author mentions the importance of cultural competency in mental health professionals and the challenges faced when providers lack understanding or relatability. How can training programs better equip future therapists and counselors to provide sensitive, empathetic care to diverse populations?

REFLECTION QUESTIONS

2. The cyclical nature of OCD can feel inescapable. What science-based tools or strategies resonated with you as potential avenues for breaking this cycle and reclaiming control over one's thoughts and behaviors?

REFLECTION QUESTIONS

3. This chapter explores the idea of reframing OCD as a gift rather than a curse, and how it can cultivate "sage powers" like empathy, exploration, innovation, and resilience. How might adopting this perspective be beneficial for all mental health challenges?

_____

_____

_____

_____

_____

_____

_____

_____

_____

_____

_____

_____

Chapter 6 | Dr. Cheryl Cooper

No Dark-Skinned Woman, You are Not the Same as Her

**Trigger Warning: This chapter discusses sexual assault and may not be suitable for all readers.

> *First, they ignore you, then they laugh at you, then they fight you, then you win.*
>
> —Mahatma Gandhi

Introduction

My story begins as a Black woman in the military, dealing with heartbreak and loss. I turned to alcohol to numb my pain, which led to an acquaintance named Clyde sexually assaulting me while my young daughter slept nearby.

He threatened to kill my daughter if she awoke and saw him and decided later to tell someone.

Mental health is critically important for overall well-being, yet it is often overlooked, especially in marginalized communities. My experiences with trauma and the lack of adequate mental health support highlight the need for greater awareness and compassionate care.

When I finally reported the assault to military police, they brought in outside law enforcement since Clyde was a civilian. I had met him at one of the nightclubs that I frequented. I would usually run into him on Wednesday or Friday nights.

He was also hanging on the walls at the club, checking all the girls out. I never saw him with anyone that would indicate he had a girlfriend; he was just a regular at the club. He introduced himself to me and asked me to dance one night. Clyde knew several other people at the clubs so I figured he must be cool; no one that I should fear.

Because I had so little information about where he lived or to identify him, the police never found him. Clyde was never charged for assaulting me.

My contact with military counseling after the assault was painful and added insult to injury. I encountered a white female counselor who seemed dismissive, looking away and rolling her eyes as I detailed my trauma.

As a Black woman, I felt my pain was seen as less important than a white woman's would be. My tears and cries for help were ignored, continuing a long, historical pattern of suppressing Black women's voices and humanity. Statistics confirm Black women are less likely to be believed in cases of sexual assault. After feeling unheard in counseling, I turned to alcohol to cope.

My story illustrates how intersecting biases of race and gender can prevent Black women from receiving compassionate mental health support after trauma. I felt vilified, dehumanized, and blamed for my own assault. However, I found power in realizing that I must take control of my life and healing. Though challenged, I remained grateful and determined to overcome what happened.

This chapter illustrates the double jeopardy that Black women face, as articulated by Frances Beal in her influential 1969 essay "Black Women's Manifesto; Double Jeopardy: To Be Black and Female."1 Beal explained that Black women suffer from intersecting oppressions due to both their race and gender, stating "Black women are tried twice for the crime of existing."

My story aligns with Beal's analysis, as she felt dehumanized and vilified by her counselor's racist and sexist perceptions. Her pain was minimized due to being both Black and female.

The lack of compassion the author received continues a long history of dismissing Black women's voices, humanity, and trauma. As Beal wrote, Black women are engaged in a daily struggle against exploitation and prejudice.

The fact that my counselor did not take my crisis seriously reflects the double standards still faced by Black women seeking health care and other services. My womanhood was weaponized against me, as it fed into harmful stereotypes about Black women's supposed promiscuity.

The lack of trauma-informed care shown in this story represents a wider problem that mental health providers must acknowledge and address. All people, regardless of race, gender or background, deserve to have their pain heard and supported on the journey to healing. Increased education, awareness and compassion for diverse perspectives is needed to provide equitable mental health treatment for all.

CHOICES UNRAVELED

I was stationed in Hawaii, and my heart was broken after my husband's death. I would occasionally go to Waikiki, to a bar to have a drink and dance to get things off my mind and numb my pain. I would spend time with locals who were nonmilitary.

Many local residents, both men and women, became friends, and I would invite them to my home or would call them to meet up with at a bar. I had a great relationship with my babysitter who lived in the same apartment complex, so she would watch my daughter whenever I wanted to go out.

One night after too much drinking and a lot of dancing, I headed home. When I got to my apartment, I ran up the stairs to my neighbor's residence and picked up my little girl and put her to bed. Minutes later, there was a knock at my front door.

It was Clyde. I didn't even know Clyde knew where I lived. I opened the door.

"What's up?" I asked.

"Can I come in?"

I obliged, saying, "Come on in," as I waved him through the door. "How do you know where I live?"

"I followed you to your house. I like you."

Clyde following me spooked me out, but I felt more comfortable while we talked about stuff that wasn't important at the dining room table.

After a while, I opened a bottle of cognac and poured us a drink. We talked and laughed some more before we stumbled back to my bedroom where I turned on the radio. As we sat on the bed continuing to talk, Clyde leaned in to kiss me and grabbed my breast. I remember pulling back and asking him what he was doing.

"Man, are you crazy?"

He did not take no for an answer. We struggled with each other on the bed as I repeatedly asked him to get off me and I yelled several foul words. I screamed at him to stop, but he violently threw my arms above my head and slammed me on the floor.

I was sexually and physically assaulted, then locked in a closet while my daughter slept in her room. He released me the next day and said if I told anyone, he would kill my daughter. I just sat through that next day feeling hopeless as thoughts raced through my head, thinking he must have planned this all along.

They are all innocent until proven guilty. But not me, I'm a liar until I am proven honest. - Louise O'Neil, Asking for it.

Mommy's in the Closet

The Navy classified my assault as a nonmilitary rape because Clyde was a civilian, but it was still rape.

I didn't think something like this would happen to military people. Locked in a closet for hours, traumatized while my daughter slept in the other room. I recall my supervisor calling my house because I had not shown up to work.

My daughter, according to a military report made, answered the phone, and said, "Mommy is locked in the bedroom." My daughter spoke through the door that someone wanted me on the phone.

Clyde fled shortly before the authorities arrived at my home. I reported the incident to the Navy military police, but when they asked for his name, I froze. When the police asked me for his name again, I told them I didn't know, nor did I have an address. I was scared, afraid of what Clyde would do the next time he saw me, and I was afraid for my baby.

Since Clyde was a civilian, outside police were contacted and took an incident report. It was horrible having to relive how I knew Clyde, how long I knew him, where he lived, why I let a stranger in my house, and if I encouraged him. Heck, I didn't even know Clyde's last name or where he lived. He was never found or prosecuted. With little information for the police to find Clyde, there were no criminal charges.

I just wanted it all to stop. It wasn't physical pain I felt but the deepening pain of shame which solidified my lack of self-worth. My world shifted just when I thought I was getting myself together. It didn't seem fair.

I Cried Again When the White Women Raped Me

I hadn't experienced racism in the military before the rape, but I got a front-row seat after my assault. Whenever I caught the counselor looking away or rolling her eyes, she reminded me that my pain, cries, and hurt as a Black woman were meaningless. I didn't feel like opening and bearing my soul to a counselor who, through her demeanor, couldn't care less what I had to say.

This particular counselor was not sympathetic. I felt like she looked at me as another woman who said no but really wanted it. During one session, I poured out my heart, as she fumbled around her desk and took a personal phone call.

The myth that Black women don't cry because they are resilient and strong is not true. Even though my tears flowed mercilessly, my words fell on deaf ears. I cried again as I felt my inner soul being violated and raped over and over.

The Black woman's voice has been suppressed for hundreds of years, as evidenced by the soft whispers of Black women speaking about their stories behind closed doors of being beaten and raped by men and even law enforcement. If a Black woman's tears carried the same weight as a white woman's, then I would have received the same compassion and recognition.

I felt she was just doing her job and really didn't care about what I had gone through. I told her what she wanted to hear and held back the tears. Her lack of attention to what I was saying told me she still believed the old myth that Black women are promiscuous and hypersexual, or that I deserved it.

The myth is still believed by far too many today. They judged me to be guilty, for one, because of double jeopardy and intersectionality by being a woman with brown skin. Statistics show Black women are less likely to be believed compared to white women in cases of rape. Furthermore, from a report from Georgetown Law Center on Poverty and Equality, white people don't see the humanity or innocence of the Black girl (The Georgetown Law Center on Poverty and Inequality, 2022).

After reading the report, I felt vilified. She looked at me as less than a human, as though the stereotypes of Black women being dehumanized through enslavement and forced into sexual coercion were just a part of life. Even though my sexual assault occurred long after the end of enslavement, I believe, based on the rolling of her blue eyes, that she thought I shouldn't be upset because the rape was what I should expect. It was after my counseling sessions I found peace in a drink of whiskey that helped me get through the day, after I felt my tears and voice were being ignored.

This was another low point in my life. I thought often about what I needed to do as I struggled to find someone I trusted to talk to and share how hopeless I felt. But something inside me wanted to fight. I told myself that I couldn't let this destroy my life and was determined to build upon my pain and make some changes in my life.

I found my power in finally understanding I was the key to deciding what I wanted to do with my life. Where I spent my time, how I chose to respond, and where I invested my energy both physically or emotionally; that was where I would reap the rewards or gain nothing.

Nobody could help me but me. I realized I still had plenty to be grateful for. My greatest challenge in life would be to fix me.

I later obtained help from a different psychiatrist and continued to receive counseling from the military. It was a service they offered, and I needed someone to talk to as I continued to struggle to concentrate, and I was having nightmares.

Otherwise, I suffered in silence mostly because I was too afraid to share with others that I wasn't coping well with life. I woke at night screaming or because I could not breathe and I was always looking over my shoulder. It was a muzzled suffering because there were no other people I could tell. I eventually stopped going to see the therapist again because I didn't feel she understood or wanted to help me.

For every Black woman who reports a rape, fifteen women do not report their assault, according to the American Psychological Association (Barlow, 2020). Black women have historically experienced higher levels of sexual and psychological abuse over all other women, which supports the reality of the Black woman's institutionalized oppression.

When a Black woman is raped and reports it, there is inclusivity of applying the law at the onset of criminal charges, but the Black woman neither receives the same equity of compassionate treatment nor the equal application of the law. My immediate supervisor, military health professionals, and chains of command in the military failed to protect me as demonstrated by the little support I received in my care after the assault and rape.

They victimized me all over again and so I began to cut myself to release my pain. My tears faded in pain through my blood from the cuts. First starting with minor cuts on my thighs so I could hide the scars while in the military. I hid my secret with smiles from people who looked at me but didn't see me.

Find a place inside where there's joy, and the joy will burn out the pain. ~ Joseph Campbell (1904 – 1987) An American writer, Campbell was also a professor of literature at Sarah Lawrence College.

PADDED CELL: LOCKED UP FOR SEEKING HELP

After my honorable discharge from the military following eight years of service, I came home with mixed emotions. It had been a little over a year since someone killed my husband. To learn more about Bishop, I discuss him in more detail in my memoir, Hood to Hooded.

This would be my first time back in Kansas City since his funeral. He was gone, and I was unsure about what my life would look like.

When I arrived, I was 28 years old and a little excited, looking forward to a fresh start. I was older. I had grown up and was more mature after serving my country.

I decided to pursue opportunities in the private sector. With a love for technology I learned from my military service, I gravitated towards Internet

Service Providers (ISP), a significant part of the telecommunication industry and landed a job with a major Fortune 100 telecommunications company.

I also established myself as a civilian and used the medical services provided by the Veterans Administration (VA) hospital. While at the veteran's hospital many years later for treatment of a recurring dislocated shoulder, I was still struggling to cope with life and mentioned to my primary doctor the sexual assault. I shared that Clyde had raped me a decade prior. She asked if I would like to speak with someone, explaining that the VA had services to help women who were sexually assaulted while on duty.

Jumping at the chance to have someone help me, I agreed. I met with a psychiatrist within weeks.

When I arrived, there were several other veterans there, most of them men. I quietly sat there in a corner until my name was called. When I got in the exam room, the doctor asked me a series of questions about my past, how things were going, and how I was coping. I can't recall all the questions he asked, but I do remember what he said next.

"Have you ever tried to hurt or kill yourself?"

When I replied, "Yes," the conversation quickly changed.

"I think it will be good for you to spend just a couple days here."

"I have to work tomorrow."

"We will take care of that. We'll let you call your place of work."

"Can I go have a cigarette first before you admit me?"

"Just wait right here. I'll be back."

As he walked out the door, I waited a few seconds and looked out the door for anyone who might be in the hallway. I walked out of the room and proceeded toward the front exit of the hospital. As I walked down the corridor to the front door, the doctor called out my name.

"Stop, Cheryl, come back here."

I turned around, looked back, and picked up the pace to a quick step. I continued to move toward the front door exit. I was sure not to run as I did not want to draw attention or come across anyone who may try to stop me. As he caught up to me at the revolving doors, he stuck his foot in the door that would not allow me to go through the revolving doors.

With my heart pounding, I quickly scanned my environment and noticed there was a single door just several feet away. I dashed toward it, ran out and continued a quick pace with the doctor following only a few feet behind.

I came to a stop just outside the door and reached inside my purse. I grabbed a cigarette from my cigarette pack, stuck it in my mouth and lit it as I stood outside the front door with the doctor standing at my side. I inhaled that cigarette and blew it out as he stood and watched.

I soon saw someone in a blue uniform standing outside the corner of my eye and quickly realized it was a police officer. Trembling, I continued to smoke my cigarette. I was angry that the hospital wanted to admit me to the psychiatric ward and refused to let me leave.

"Why did you leave?" the doctor asked.

"I told you I wanted a cigarette."

"Are you okay?"

"I can't stop shaking."

"Why is that? Why are you shaking?"

"You made me so angry because all I wanted was a cigarette," I answered. "I'm trembling because I'm holding my rage inside as I'm trying to deal with how you're treating me."

As the doctor stood there staring at me, he stood in silence as the police officer continued to wait for instructions. I thought they must think I'm crazy. What could I possibly have said to make the doctor take such extreme actions as to call the police for assistance? What have I gotten myself into? I continued to puff on my cigarette, inhaling and slowly exhaling as I tried to calm the fury inside me.

After I flipped the cigarette into the grass, I turned to the doctor and said, "I'm ready."

I walked back through the hospital double doors with the doctor and the police officer following behind. As we approached the elevators to go up to the tenth floor where the psych ward was located, the doctor waved the police officer away indicating he didn't need his assistance. That day they locked me up in a psych ward for two days, unable to leave, or even walk outside for a breath of fresh air.

THE BIG CUT

Over many years, I cut myself to help me cope with my rape. I think it grew into a habit, like an alcohol or a drug addiction. Why would anyone cut or hurt themselves because it sounds crazy, right? People think it's a cry for help, but I usually cut in silence. Mostly, I cut my legs or the thighs because I didn't want people to know. The only time I needed help was when I cut too deep and needed someone to help stitch me up. I then went about my business and went to work the next day.

I was an educated professional with a thriving career, so what was the big deal, right? Few people know that I'm a cutter, mainly just my doctors. Sometimes the cutting is because I want to stop hurtingv... stop the tears... stop the headaches ... stop the pain... stop the despair and anguish. Pacing the floor and walking up and down the stairs, sometimes I cannot shake the feeling inside my body that is like a bug crawling through my skin.

One time, I called the suicide hotline because I continued to feel that way, even after trying to talk my way through it. After I hung up the phone, I grabbed the razor and I cut, cut, cut ...as I had done many times before. Then other times I cut for no reason. It made me feel good — a rush, like getting high. I got so used to cutting, I would put razor blades on my grocery store shopping list to make sure I always had some on hand.

Many times, I cut myself because I hated myself. I have made so many mistakes, and hurt so many other people, I felt I deserved the bloody pain.

Emotional pain can live on for what seems like an eternity. A physical razor slice of the wrists and the emotional pain is gone. I continued to see several psychiatrists for a few years and was later medically diagnosed with post-traumatic stress disorder (PTSD).

The Pivot

Seeking help from the VA, I realized I didn't have my shit together like I thought. There was a part of me I refused to acknowledge for years because it was too painful. It was like refusing to grieve, allowing my hurt to fester into uncontrollable destructive darkness. The trauma and the oppression are things I am always actively overcoming. Still under a doctor's care, I'm learning to use my life to help others to rise. I choose to do the hard work on myself to heal, so I can be of greater service to my community.

I learned that sometimes we have to find something bigger than us to begin healing. I aspire to make the world a better place for those who look like me and may have had similar oppressive and traumatic experiences I've had, especially women of color. I thrive and no longer define myself as a victim of what has happened to me or the choices I made when I was younger. The choices I made in the past helped me to be wiser.

I learned that even though we can't control what happens to us, we don't have to let it limit us. Recovering from sexual assault takes time, and the healing process can be painful. But we can regain our sense of control, rebuild our self-worth, and learn to heal.

Dr. Cheryl Cooper

Dr. Cheryl Cooper, a United States Navy veteran and Doctor of Computer Science, is a trailblazing cybersecurity leader, author, speaker, and information security officer with an impressive 25-year career. Her innovative strategies empower companies to cultivate diverse cyber talent, fostering a culture of innovation that drives profitability.

As a charismatic and sought-after speaker, Dr. Cooper fearlessly addresses the multifaceted aspects of cybersecurity. Through her groundbreaking books, "Hood to Hooded" and "Triumph in the Trenches: Navigating Success for Black Professionals," she candidly shares her personal journey of empowerment through choice. By openly discussing the traumas she endured, Dr. Cooper ignites her purpose to create change in systems that oppress women. Her powerful messages, "Emancipation of the Mind" and "Streets to Suites," inspire audiences to break free from limitations and step into their greatness.

Driven by her frustration with the lack of engagement from potential role models and mentors in her community, Dr. Cooper founded the non-profit organization Women in CyberSecurity (Affiliate) of the greater Kansas City, Missouri, and Kansas Metroplex. Through her tireless efforts, she has championed hundreds of underserved high school students, organizing field trips to technology companies across Kansas City, Seattle, and Dallas. Her goal is to provide visibility and representation, enabling young people to envision themselves thriving in the world.

She has received multiple awards, including the Central Exchange Midwest Award for being a woman's champion and bridge builder, as well as the Martin Luther King, Jr. Award for "Keeping the Dream Alive" in education and community service. Dr. Cooper's mission is clear: "We must see the Black and Brown girl in a world in which she is usually unseen."

Dr. Cooper is dedicated to making the change she didn't see and passing on the baton of empowerment to future generations.

REFLECTION QUESTIONS

1. The author turned to self-harm to cope with her trauma and pain. While this provided temporary relief, it ultimately caused more harm. What healthy coping mechanisms could one pursue to process their emotions?

REFLECTION QUESTIONS

2. The author's story highlights the intersecting oppression and "double jeopardy" Black women face due to their race and gender. How does this intersectionality impact mental health and access to equitable care? What can be done to break down these intersecting biases and stigmas?

___

___

___

___

___

___

___

___

___

___

___

___

___

___

___

REFLECTION QUESTIONS

3. The author states "I learned that our circumstances don't define who we are... we decide who we want to be through our actions." How can reframing one's mindset from victimhood to empowerment aid the healing process after trauma? What life lessons or wisdom from the author resonated most with you?

Chapter 7 | Bridgette Nelson
Suppression of the High-Functioning Black Woman

> *I'm tackling the myth that African-American women have to be pillars of strength. We have the right to fall. We have the right not to always have our sh*t together.*
>
> —Lisa Nicole Carson

As American's, we've endured a long-standing conditioning to persist in our progress despite the numerous challenges we encounter. We push down our feelings of deep generational pain and trauma in pursuit of the American dream and, ultimately, survival.

The truth is mental health should be a high priority for every human being carrying the mental load of surviving life. At some point in their lives, more than 50% of Americans in the United States will be diagnosed with a mental illness or disorder.[1] This is due in large part to life's adversities, medical conditions, biological or chemical imbalances in the brain, substance abuse, trauma, and harmful emotions.

It's no wonder why, during the pandemic, we saw a major increase in anxiety and depression in comparison to previous years.[2] With layoffs,

---

[1] Kessler RC, Angermeyer M, Anthony JC, et al. Lifetime prevalence and age-of-onset distributions of mental disorders in the World Health Organization's World Mental Health Survey Initiative. World Psychiatry. 2007;6(3):168-176.

[2] Tackling the mental health impact of the COVID-19 crisis: An integrated, whole of society response. OECD.

isolation, and being quarantined left with no distractions or work, we were all left to listen to the ringing sounds of all of those dark emotions and harsh realities we've tried hard to forget. pushed down.

America, one of the most progressive countries in the world, still cannot accomplish universal healthcare, let alone mental health. Employment is the most prominent means of accessing healthcare, and employer-sponsored benefits or employee assistance programs provide the majority of mental health care coverage.[1]

Amid the COVID-19 pandemic and current climatic recession, it is even more important for employers to be aware, as there is a serious impact on not only the individual but also organizational costs. This is due to the link between mental health and its impact on workplace productivity, which includes absenteeism, presenteeism, workplace accidents, employee attrition, workers insurance claims, and litigation.[2] In addition, the workplace can often provide an environment for the creation of conditions that amplify mental health stress, known as work-related stress. These conditions are associated with poor supervision, high job demands, conflict, a lack of resources, etc., and can ultimately result in negative job satisfaction and burnout.[3]

---

[1] Chen, Y., Chu, H., & Wang, P. (2021). Employee assistance programs: A meta-analysis. Journal of Employment Counseling, 58(4), 144–166. https://doi.org/10.1002/joec.12170

[2] Hilton, M., Sheridan, J., Cleary, C., & Whiteford, H. (2009). Employee absenteeism measures reflecting current work practices may be instrumental in a re-evaluation of the relationship between Psychological distress/mental health and absenteeism. International journal of methods in psychiatric research. 18. 37-47. 10.1002/mpr.275.

[3] Khamisa N, Oldenburg B, Peltzer K, Ilic D. Work related stress, burnout, job satisfaction and general health of nurses. Int J Environ Res Public Health. 2015 Jan 12;12(1):652-66. doi: 10.3390/ijerph120100652. PMID: 25588157; PMCID: PMC4306884.

Now, let's add the layer of race to the equation: a historically marginalized race. Black people. The theoretical framework used to understand the systemic influences that impact the psychological experiences of Black people is the multisystem/racial identity model. This model shows how systemic oppression, which is made up of dominant cultural patterns, controls how people think and feel, how families work, how money is spent, and how communities are run.[1]

Specifically, BIPOC communities experience a higher degree of life adversity than white communities, stemming from the effects of systemic racism. Race-based traumatic stress (RBTS), a mental and emotional injury resulting from encounters with racial bias, ethnic discrimination, racism, and hate crimes, can manifest itself.[2] This leaves Black people especially susceptible to experiencing a mental illness or disorder.

Let's make it plain. We, as a people enslaved on stolen land, have laboriously built this nation, demanding reparations, justice, and equality even after more than 400 years. We have generational traumas of racism, colorism, sexual abuse, addiction, mass incarceration, discrimination, and the ultimate decline of the black family. People have conditioned us to view our mental health as a secondary concern. It doesn't matter if you are tired, hurt, or scarred; you keep picking that cotton. You're tougher than your emotions. Bury them. Hide them. Keep wearing the mask.

---

[1] Franklin, A.J., Carter, R.T., Grace, C. (1993). An Integrative Approach to Psychotherapy with Black/African Americans. In: Stricker, G., Gold, J.R. (eds) Comprehensive Handbook of Psychotherapy Integration. Springer, Boston, MA.

[2] Carter, Robert T. "Race-Based Traumatic Stress." Psychiatric Times, vol. 23, no. 14, 1 Dec. 2006, p. 37. Gale OneFile: Health and Medicine, link.gale.com/apps/doc/A156586128/HRCA?u=anon~1b6628d0&sid=googleScholar&xid=cc39616f.

Well, I'm here to say that it's time to take the mask off. Here is how I came to discover it for myself.

She raised me with remarkable resilience. Her story is not mine to tell, so I won't, but her story has greatly influenced mine. There are many things I have learned from this woman that, in my later years, I have grown tremendously appreciative of. And yet, that was not always the case. For most of us, trauma begins at home, sometimes directly and sometimes indirectly. Sometimes intentionally, and sometimes unintentionally.

As a child, I watched my mom play the role of caretaker and provider. She was a hard woman, with few words or affection. My father, a good and well intentioned man, struggled with job security. He had a hard exterior, but he was a big softie, the nurturer of my two parents. They divorced when I was a child, and I remember the day it all came to a head so vividly. They argued all day, while my sisters and I stayed in our rooms. They've argued before, as most couples do. I mean, for a brief period of time, I believed that discarding burritos from the freezer was a healthy way to release aggression when one was angry. But this day felt different. My sister and I stayed in our room, but our faces were filled with worry. The air was thick. Later that night, Mom woke us up and told us we were leaving. The neighbors called the police, and as I woke up, I could see red and blue lights flashing outside the window. My dad was running down the stairs, pleading, and my mom was gathering items to pack up to leave. I was 7 years old. Scared. Crying hysterically. They divorced. They broke our family.

Afraid to bring it up to my mom, I tried talking with my older sister about it. She shut me out of having those types of conversations and dealt with them herself. It was then that I learned to suppress the hard, difficult, and emotional stuff. Something we watched our mother do into adulthood, and so we did it too. It was a learned behavior. As the years passed by, I continued to experience what I know now to be the traumas that helped shape my self-perspective. Seeing nigger spray painted on our new condo, being the only black kid in class at a predominately white school and community, being the loner fat kid in the family with Miss Popular Homecoming Queen for a big sister and the cute, charming kid for a little sister, made fun of at school, and trying to figure out who the heck you are. I learned to shut it down, push it down, and do your work to make it through life.

These experiences, as well as the resulting feelings and mental stories I created as a child, compounded on one another, lying dormant to the naked eye underneath the surface of what I chose to expose the world to. As I grew older and continued to bury my emotions, I instead devoted myself to becoming the picture-perfect, high-functioning black woman. I developed codependent behaviors of seeking validation through works. I threw myself into academics, never getting anything less than an A and graduating at the top of my class in grade school and junior high. In high school, I was class vice president for 3 years, took advanced classes, mentored underclassmen, played basketball, graduated with a 4.4 GPA, went on to attend USC, became a resident advisor for 4 years, pledged a sorority, graduated with a good-paying job that allowed me to travel, and married my college sweetheart. I developed great relationships with people, pouring so much into relationships and things, that I often neglected myself. And I didn't even know it because I had everything I needed, on the outside.

The picture was perfect, or was it? In 2016, I faced eviction from my apartment. While out running errands with my mom and my 1-year-old daughter, I got a phone call from the police regarding our apartment lockout. While my eyes glazed with bewilderment, I stopped in my tracks. Lockout? Eviction? How could this be? When we had our daughter, my husband and I decided I would stay home to raise her. I was an excited new mother, and I could not bring myself to go back to work, leaving her. After all, I had been carrying us financially for years and was ready to hand over the reins. I immediately called my husband after I got off the phone with the officer. He sighed and admitted that we were behind on our rent, but he thought he had more time. Time ran out. We had until 6 o'clock that evening to get all of our stuff out of the apartment. Devastated. Betrayed. Blind-sided. He kept this from me. And so we go again. He broke our family.

The next few years were tough — adjusting to parenthood, parenting parents, jobs, and marital misalignment. But things got better. Fast forward to 2019. I had just received a promotion at the company I fell in love with on my return to the workforce; I had started graduate school; and my husband had finally landed a job that would help his career. We just gave birth to the final piece of our family puzzle: our son. And for some reason, I could not shake the feelings. The picture was perfect, right? So many emotions I had suppressed over the years were all there on the surface. As much as I tried to high-function them away, they left me functionally paralyzed. I returned to work eight weeks after having my son, and I was not mentally ready. I was suicidal, and after a month and an intimate conversation with my boss, it became apparent that it was time to address what was underneath the surface. I was a high-functioning, depressed black woman, and I was barely holding on.

At the time, I had very limited mental health coverage under my medical benefits. Our employee-assistance program (EAP) resources only sponsored six sessions, necessitating out-of-pocket payment for additional sessions. Additionally, I knew that if I needed to address my mental wellbeing, it needed to be with a person who looked like me and could understand my experiences — a black woman (most of us are high-functioning). Fortunately, my professor connected me with my therapist, but her private practice meant I would have to cover all the costs myself. Ultimately, I decided it was worth it because she came highly recommended, I was in need, and with the new promotion income, I could afford it.

This was one of the best decisions I have made in my life. Motherhood is a big part of my identity, and how could I help raise whole people if I wasn't whole myself? I realized that in order for me to truly be the kind of mother I wanted to be, I had to reckon with the unhealed parts of my childhood and adult experiences. Our experiences shape our ideologies, standards of being, and subsequent behaviors. Therapy allowed me time to reflect, consider, and really question these things. I had to confront my deepest thoughts so I could make room for clarity and insights and develop strategies for healthy management moving forward. As a high-functioning black woman, wellness became a new aspect of my identity and profession.

As we navigate mental health and the offerings available to us via the workplace, is America equitably caring for and retaining the productivity of our Black communities?

Access is the biggest barrier to mental health utilization. In a study by Le Cook et al. a three-component framework was offered for understanding factors that impact utilization: characteristics of the health care delivery system (e.g., the market share of health maintenance organizations), enabling community-level variables (e.g., the supply of local providers), and external environmental factors (e.g., socioeconomic conditions).[1] Le Cook's findings indicated that utilization disparities were most influenced by provider supply.[2] In particular, when it comes to workplace healthcare benefits provider supply, employees are restricted to using a network of professionals approved by their organization's benefits package. The Substance Abuse and Mental Health Services Administration (SAMHSA) predicted that by 2025, shortages of more than 236,000 mental health professionals across the specialties of marriage and family therapy, psychiatry, mental health counseling, social work, psychology, and school counseling would be experienced.[3] As my own story tells you, studies have also indicated that Black people prefer to receive care from Black therapists who share their cultural lived experience. This creates a huge problem when only 17% of the US psychology field is ethnically identified as BIPOC, and the smallest proportion of this population consists of Black clinicians, which comprise only 3% of the field.

Cost is another issue. While getting exercise by going for a walk may incur no cost, mental health wellbeing services can typically get quite costly, amounting to $100–200 on average for a single psychotherapy session.[4] I

---

[1] Le Cook, B., Doksum, T., Chen, C., Carle, A., & Alegría, M. (2013). The role of provider supply and organization in reducing racial/ethnic disparities in mental health care in the U.S. Social Science & Medicine, 84, 102–109. https://doi.org/10.1016/j.socscimed.2013.02.006

[2] Carbral, R. R., & Smith, T. B. (2011). Racial/ethnic matching of clients and therapists in mental health services: A meta-analytic review of preferences, perceptions, and outcomes. Journal of Counseling Psychology, 58(4), 537–554

[3] Substance Abuse and Mental Health Services Administration. (SAMHSA). (2021, October). Key substance use and mental health indicators in the United States: Results from the 2020 National Survey on Drug Use and Health. Center for Behavioral Health Statistics and Quality. https://www.samhsa.gov/data/sites/default/files/reports/rpt35325/NSDUHFFRPDFWHTMLFiles2020/2020NSDUHFFR1PDFW102121.pdf

[4] Lauretta, A. (2021, October 19). How much does therapy cost? Forbes. https://www.forbes.com/health/mind/how-much-does-therapy-cost/

can vouch for this personally. While individuals may use health insurance benefits to reduce their out-of-pocket expenses, insurance plans usually restrict the number of sessions permitted, the services they cover, and the providers they can use.

Now let's address the elephant in the room. It is no secret that there is a controversial stigma and attitude surrounding mental illness in the Black community. This, coupled with the minimization of mental health as an issue, proves a challenge for Black people to feel safe sharing psychological symptoms.[1] Instead, we choose not to talk about it because feelings of trauma are a sign of weakness, and that is one thing a Black person will never show. Moreover, Black communities often place greater reliance on religious faith as a sole source for combating mental health challenges. My faith was also a big part of my healing. But, we are taught to solely rely on God and pray to Him for our healing, but in order for that to work, we also have to do the work inside.

So how do we normalize wellness within the Black community? Traditionally, a third-party vendor has managed and offered most mental health resources or behavioral health services as a standalone package, separate from the primary medical plan.[2] Black people prefer primary healthcare utilization of mental health or behavioral health services as a way of normalizing it with general health care.[3] Therefore, I urge

---

[1] Arday, J. (2022). No one can see me cry: Understanding mental health issues for black and minority ethnic staff in higher education. Higher Education, 83(1), 79–102. https://doi.org/10.1007/s10734-020-00636-w

[2] Maeng, D., Cornell, A. E., & Nasra, G. S. (2021). Employer-sponsored behavioral health program impacts on care utilization and cost. American Journal of Managed Care, 27(8), 812–817. https://doi.org/10.1097/JOM.0000000000001678

[3] Kawaii-Bogue, B., Williams, N. J., & MacNear, K. (2017). Mental health care access and treatment utilization in African American communities: An integrative care framework. Best Practices in Mental Health: An International Journal, 13(2), 11–29.

employers to offer mental health care options that are both low-cost and free, and to manage them in the same manner as primary healthcare. Secondly, Black people need their choice of providers, and the access to and availability of Black clinicians must be dramatically increased. I encourage you, if you're considering a career in mental health! We need you.

To the woman who is juggling it all, has it all, or is barely surviving: I see you. In my journey of overcoming postpartum depression, I unearthed that I was a high-functioning depressed person throughout the majority of my life. And there are so many other women just like me. I pray that we stop burying our darkest emotions and turn them into convicted vulnerabilities for triumphant victory. Every time I got on a plane to travel for work, I'd overhear the flight attendant tell the mom sitting with her child, "In the case of a flight emergency and the oxygen masks are deployed, place the mask over yourself first before you assist others." It is now a motto I try my best to live by now. My purpose on this earth is to help others, and I choose to always check my oxygen mask first, so that I can be of good use to the world. Therapy helped me to do just that. I hope that you will also choose to listen to your own voice of wellness.

BRIDGETTE NELSON

Bridgette Nelson, an expert in learning and organization development, holds a bachelor's degree in business administration from the University of Southern California and a Master's Degree in Organization Development from Pepperdine University. She has built a career transforming organizations through its people.

https://www.jaxsongrowth.com.

REFLECTION QUESTIONS

1. How does the author's journey illustrate the complex interplay between personal experiences, cultural influences, and systemic barriers in accessing mental health care?

Reflection Questions

2. How does the author's former coping mechanisms, such as high achievement and suppression of emotions, reflect common responses to trauma? How might these coping strategies impact long-term mental health and well-being?

REFLECTION QUESTIONS

3. What steps can be taken at both the individual and institutional levels to address disparities in mental health services and support marginalized individuals in their healing journey?

_____

_____

_____

_____

_____

_____

_____

_____

_____

_____

_____

_____

_____

_____

Chapter 8 | Elona Washington

Searching for Safety
Piecing Together a Shattered Past

**Trigger Warning: This chapter discusses suicide and sexual abuse and may not be suitable for all readers.

Frankie's not here. She's awake and frightened. I'm getting tired of having to step in for her...

—Frankie Murdoch [as her alter-ego Alice] from the movie *Frankie & Alice*

Ever since I could remember, the voices in my head have been constant companions. As a child, they were my playmates. While family members assumed I was talking to myself when I braided Barbie's hair or built cabins with Lincoln Logs, in reality, I was hosting playdates with imaginary friends. As I grew older, the innocent chatter of my childhood companions became more serious, reflecting the increasing challenge for my safety.

The quest for safety has been the undercurrent of my life, influencing every decision, every relationship, and every struggle. It pushed me to continuously seek out new havens, like relocating to different cities every few years. But despite every attempt I made, every decision resulted in toxic situations, as I couldn't stop mistaking the familiar for the safe.

And the voices were sick of it.

SAFE IS NOT THE OPPOSITE OF DANGER

Why you letting her come?
You know we don't like her.
Don't you remember what she did to us?

The voices would not stop talking. Each had their own unique pitch and tone. Some sounded like a little girl, and others, a grown-ass teenager. Sometimes, they talked to each other about silly things. And sometimes they spoke directly to me. When they spoke to me, it was usually to correct me, remind me of a past mistake, or worse.

This time, the voices were chattering incessantly and louder than ever. I landed a dream marketing job, but even before I started, I knew things were going to be awful. I had gotten two job offers at a Big 5 Publisher: one with a wonderful manager, and during our interview, we ended up chatting casually about books. The other? During our phone interview, she rarely gave me a chance to speak. She droned on about her accomplishments and how she was so great. When she turned the conversation back to the interview process, she noted that she was impressed by my resume but added, "I know people lie on their resumes to get the job. It seems like you've done a lot; I just want to make sure that if I bring you on, you can do everything that's on here."

When we ended our call, I immediately called a mutual acquaintance to recount the conversation. I was incensed, offended, and felt my integrity and professionalism attacked. The voices in my head were going off! They told me not to choose her offer. For days, that was all they would say. Throughout my entire life, I always ignored them, and this time was no different. I made the decision to work under a toxic boss. I know. I know.

From the very first day, my nervous system was on high alert. It wasn't long before I grew defensive in meetings, then eventually shut down altogether. But something inside wanted to prove to my manager that I was good enough. From where does such longing come? You guessed it. An unresolved relationship with a parent; in this case, my mother.

Growing up, safety was an elusive concept. My home, which should have been a sanctuary, felt like a minefield of unlove, dislike, and criticism. While the people in my life tried excusing my mother's behavior toward me, one day, in my early 30s, I received confirmation that my mother did not like me. She told me, "I love you because I have to, but I don't like you. And I don't understand why my two favorite people in the world speak so highly of you." She was referring to my grandmother and stepfather.

Sigmund Freud would explain that my experiences with my mother and making the conscious choice to work with a toxic boss demonstrate repetition compulsion, which is characterized by unconsciously recreating early trauma. I unconsciously recreated my past by choosing a job with a toxic boss who exhibited similar behaviors as my mother—skepticism, lack of validation, and domineering communication. This unconscious recreation of trauma was, ironically, an attempt to find safety in the familiar, even if that familiarity was painful.[1]

CHILDHOOD WHISPERS

Because of our strained relationship, my son, at 17, probably saw his grandmom five times in his life. Not only did I move out of the Washington,

---

[1] Barkley, Sarah. 2022. "What Is Repetition Compulsion?" Psych Central. September 16, 2022. https://psychcentral.com/blog/repetition-compulsion-why-do-we-repeat-the-past.

DC, area shortly after he was born; when I visited my hometown, I never tried to see her. I hear y'all judging me. But trust, it went both ways.

For example, I had traveled to DC for an event and needed to stop by my mom's house for something. While I was there, I attempted to make conversation with her and my three little brothers. Shortly into the small talk only I was initiating; it was clear they wanted me to leave, so I left. About an hour later, my mom posted on Facebook that she was at the movies, and my immediate thought was, "It would have been nice if she had asked me to go." So yeah, it went both ways.

So, during my son's senior year of high school, out of the blue, my mother and sister wanted to fly to Nashville, TN to watch him play football. They asked me this a few months into my dream job with the nightmarish boss, and just the thought of my mother's visit added an additional layer of stress and self-loathing. Every voice in my head was screaming, "NOOOO! Don't let her visit!" But you guessed it. I said yes anyway. The voices were not pleased with me at all.

The time leading up to my mother's arrival was a daze. Work was demanding, I put a down payment on a house, and my son got into an at-fault accident two weeks after I bought him a car. I used the money I had set aside for closing costs to repair two cars, and I had to buckle down to save the necessary funds for closing. To say I was stressed was an understatement.

When it came time for my mother and sister to visit, I was a ball of nerves, but my sister lightened the mood with her corny jokes. I drove them to the hotel where they'd be staying for the weekend. Yes, I checked my mom into a hotel.

Homecoming weekend was fun, and we all had a wonderful time. I honestly do not recall what we did; I do not even remember picking them up and taking them to the airport. But I feel like there were no negative feelings, just awkwardness, so I assume all went well.

Despite the pleasant visit, the voices continued to rage at me. They hated mom and resented me for spending—and enjoying—time with her. On top of the daily incessant chatter, I started to have nightmares about my childhood. My closing date was a few weeks before Christmas, and the closer we got to December, the worse my life became. My son was mad at me. My daughter stopped talking to me. And my inability to sleep led to a decline in my work performance.

I thought the solution to all my problems was to focus on work. That would take my mind off my personal life. I consistently had the top-performing ads, sometimes even holding all three spots, so I had convinced myself that I wasn't doing too badly. Because I was saving, I did not want to add another expense, so I reasoned that after I closed on the house, I would get therapy.

That was the wrong decision. I was a victim of child sex abuse, and my nightmares were reliving those moments—moments I thought I had forgotten. While it was not my mom's fault and she was not the cause of the abuse, she, along with other adults in my life, knew what was happening and did nothing to protect me. Instead, they called me fast and held me accountable for the teenagers and adult men who forced me to have sex with them.

As you can see, growing up, I was not safe inside or outside the home. It took performative behavior, such as cleaning the house, cooking, watching my siblings, or just staying quiet and out of her way, to receive any praise or affection from my mother. The yelling, tension, and silent treatment weighed heavily on my underweight body. But going outside wasn't better. If my best friend's brother and his friends saw me playing in the sandbox or swinging on the tire swing, they coerced me into their house. While they promised they would not tell if I went along, they told. The accusing glances from adults and snickers from my peers caused me to withdraw. I wasn't safe anywhere.

Day in and day out, those memories and feelings flooded my system, and the voices kept repeating, "You know what she did to you," even though, honestly, I didn't. I only sensed that my mom had done something horrible during my birthday party, but I could not recall it for the life of me. My voices knew though, and they wanted nothing to do with her. The body really does keep score.

Buying the home meant everything. It was the first home I would purchase on my own, and we—the voices and I—would finally have something that we got without the help of a narcissistic husband or mean mom. However, I was unable to save enough for the closing costs, and my mother's offer to gift me the money immediately tainted our dream. "We do not want her money," they told me. But you know what I did. I accepted it anyway.

"If one more thing goes wrong, we're killing ourselves," was their message to me after making that decision. I knew they were not playing. We have made so many attempts at suicide that I could no longer count.

My therapist later explained that the reason for the voices speaking to me more regularly and sharing repressed memories in nightmares was because they believed I was ready to learn the complete truth about my past. I believe they were motivated by something else: they were tired of me choosing to feel unsafe. And yes, that included receiving money from my mother.

TOXIC BOSS, FAMILIAR DANCE

After closing, I took a two-week vacation to settle into my new home. During that time, the voices were a little quieter, maybe even a little happy. Upon my return to work, I received a calendar invitation from my boss and HR. I was being written up. While I acknowledge that I was not always present and made mistakes as a result, their solution did not address the underlying issue. My boss and HR were both aware of my past and my mental condition. I had kept them both informed about the insomnia, stress, and anxiety. While HR had suggested that I seek therapy, my boss never acknowledged the messages I sent her or held a discussion about them during our one-on-one meetings.

After laying out the performance improvement plan (PIP), I requested a private conversation with HR, reminded her of my situation, and disclosed that it had escalated to suicidal thoughts. She recommended that I go on short-term disability and tell my boss about the suicidal thoughts. HR genuinely believed that such transparency could undo the write-up or at least come up with a solution to manage my mental health during this period. The voices told me not to tell my boss that I was suicidal; but I did it anyway. My boss' response: she accused me of making it up to avoid being written up.

Now y'all see what I was dealing with? But wait. It gets worse.

The next three months were a race to see whether I could get short-term disability before being fired. And my boss set out to win by any means necessary. Having already been gaslighted and lied upon, she escalated the situation by sabotaging my work. Here's an example. She was responsible for setting the ad budget and creating the Excel sheet from where I would pull the numbers. One day, I noticed a discrepancy and asked her to fix it. She replied via email that she had fixed it, but she didn't disclose that she had also lowered the budget in other categories. During meetings, she repeatedly emphasized the importance of sharing changes to avoid mistakes, yet she purposefully failed to do so, so I would overspend.

My instincts told me to take before and after screenshots, and I did, emailing the evidence to my personal account. I also emailed her, letting her know that I knew what she did. However, I never showed the proof to her boss or HR, even though the voices were telling me to. I figured no one ever protected or believed me, so why would this be different?

To qualify for short-term disability, I needed a diagnosis and recommendation from a licensed mental health professional. After speaking with a therapist and taking a series of tests, I was diagnosed with dissociative identity disorder (DID), and we began treatment to manage the voices. While there is no prescription to cure DID or subdue the voices, she suggested that I also work with a psychiatrist to manage my depression and anxiety.

During a child's formative years, severe, prolonged trauma, significant attachment issues, or chronic neglect can trigger the development of Dissociative Identity Disorder (DID), formerly known as Multiple Personality Disorder, as a coping mechanism. It can also be characterized by the presence of two or more personality states within one individual. These separate identities, or alters, can take control of a person's thoughts, behaviors, and actions at different times. Each alter has its own unique characteristics, memories, and ways of perceiving and interacting with the world. Together, these alters comprise the individual's complete personality system.[1]

The diagnosis was frightening but I was intent on managing my alters and living a normal life. Then one morning, as I was getting ready for work, I finally understood what my alters had been trying to reveal these past few months. My sexual abuse started at two years old.

Once the revelation hit me, I had a panic attack. Unable to type, I called my boss and managed to communicate something. The next call I made was to a friend. He heard the distress in my voice and headed to my house. I do not know what I said or did when he arrived, because an alter had fronted, taken over my thoughts, behaviors, and actions. She introduced herself as Data because she liked the TV show *Star Trek Enterprise*. If I were to tell you everything else he shared, you probably wouldn't believe me. I find it hard to believe myself. What I will share is that Data and others had been fronting at work, which was why my performance suffered at times and I had no recollection of meetings or tasks. My friend even said Data reported to work a few hours after I informed my boss about the panic attack.

---

[1] Steele, Van Der Hart Nijenhuis & Kathy. 2023. "Alters in Dissociative Identity Disorder (MPD), OSDD and Partial DID." Trauma Dissociation. 2023. http://traumadissociation.com/alters.

My official diagnosis for March 2022 read:

> EW has been diagnosed with post-traumatic stress disorder, chronic (F43.12) and dissociative identity disorder (F44.81). The results of the psychological test, Multidimensional Inventory of Dissociation (MID), indicated scores that fall into the range of Post-Traumatic Stress Disorder (PTSD), Dissociative Identity Disorder, and severe attachment/ relational trauma. She was experiencing an increase in symptoms of both PTSD and DID. She experienced severe dissociation, lost orientation to time, switched between personalities or alters, blacked out, and experienced memory gaps due to these DID symptoms. EW exhibits a very limited attention span, selective inattention to emotionally charged issues, and significant amnesia. She demonstrated difficulty staying on subject, changing topics mid-sentence, and speaking tangentially. She presented with impaired retention and recall of immediate, recent, and past memories. Due to this structural amnesia, she was unable to carry out instructions (both simple and complex), complete work at a reasonable rate, interact with others appropriately, and handle the normal workload.[1]

THE SANCTUARY OF SELF

When I logged into work the next day, my boss had scheduled a meeting with me and HR. Again. It was my final warning. Once the call ended, I

---

[1] (L. Mullen, personal communication, May 24, 2022)

became manic. This was the "one more thing" the alters had warned me about.

It was a Friday night. My teenage son was upstairs, oblivious to me and my uncontrollable screaming and crying. One alter was prepared to consume the entire bottle of sleeping pills, while another objected because my son was in the house. All I could do was cry. I could not stop thinking how I had been nothing but a commodity since the age of two. How I could not hold a job. How I would have to live the rest of my life with alters. How I could never feel safe.

What prevented me from doing it was the impact it would have on my son. I managed to block out the alters and called RAINN's hotline. The rep sent an ambulance and two cop cars. All of the commotion caused one of my alters to front. She put on a brave face for the officers and neighbors who came outside to be nosy. Her acting was superb, and we successfully talked ourselves out of a trip to the psychiatric hospital. Once inside, she devised a new plan. We were going to organize our affairs and continue working to maintain our work-life insurance policy, thereby ensuring my children would receive an inheritance. Once my son started college in August, we resolved to take our life.

The next week, I met with my psychologist and psychiatrist. With a smile, laughter, and playful banter, I declared my "cure" from suicidal thoughts, requiring short-term disability to recuperate before I could resume work. My psychologist was pleased, but my psychiatrist did not buy it. He was an elderly Nigerian man who always managed to make me smile, albeit a faint one. After I shared the news and flashed my new 1000-watt smile, he simply asked, "Are you telling me the truth?" His question struck me like water hitting live wires. It jolted me to my core, short-circuiting my carefully constructed façade. Tears surged from deep within, rising through my chest and spilling over as I released a cry so heart-wrenching it felt like it was tearing my soul apart. How did he know?

During that session, I was the most vulnerable I had ever been. He increased my prescriptions and then encouraged me to open up to my psychologist. I followed his advice, and my therapist and I developed a safety plan. The Suicide Prevention Resource Center defines a safety plan as "a prioritized written list of coping strategies and sources of support that patients at high risk for suicide can utilize. The plan is brief, is in the patient's own words, and is simple to read."[1]

Remember that race between me and my boss? I won. Because of the severity of my mental health, the insurance company approved me for four months of short-term disability; I was asking for only one month. My therapist later shared that she remembered me saying, "The only way I can make these voices stop is to kill myself." She believes that statement was the driving force behind the length of time off.

During those four months, life's stressors seemed to pause. I felt lighter and more hopeful and had time to focus on my mental wellness, something I had never done before. I was the eldest daughter, a young mother, former wife, and go-to friend and family member. It never occurred to me to ever put myself first.

What was the first thing I learned to do? Rest. Working to avoid anxiety, worry, and stress was not healthy. I learned to take mental breaks to reset

---

[1] Western Interstate Commission for Higher Education, Stanley, B., PhD, & Brown, G. K. (2008). Safety Planning Guide. In Western Interstate Commission for Higher Education. https://sprc.org/wp-content/uploads/2023/01/SafetyPlanningGuide-Quick-Guide-for-Clinicians.pdf

my nervous system instead of trying to avoid negative feelings. I let the sun hit my face. I anchor myself to the earth by standing barefoot in the grass. And I finally developed the patience to practice yoga, meditate, and use sound bowls.

My therapist also taught me techniques to manage my alters, with the most important being: stop making decisions alone. When my alters cry out, it is a sign that something is wrong. Instead of rushing to fix things myself, I now pause to check if my entire system feels comfortable with the choice. This approach helps me honor the alters' concerns and has significantly improved my life, reducing internal conflicts and helping me navigate challenging situations with greater clarity and confidence. They are the ones who recall most of the abuse and the characteristics of the abusers, so it makes sense to listen to them.

The first challenging situation we had to navigate was whether I should return to work. As the time drew near, feelings of anxiety and dread returned. My alters wanted me to quit my job, but as the adult and the main front, the alter primarily in control, the thought only brought on more stress.

Then I reflected on all I had survived. The prospect of unemployment paled in comparison to all of the challenges I had overcome. So, I listened to my alters and quit that "dream job." I had no other job or clientele lined up. And it was the best decision I—no, WE—ever made.

I always wanted to start a business, so I did, finally accepting that corporate America is not for me. Here are just a few accomplishments achieved since operating an indie publishing company:

- I won a six-figure award my first year in business.
- IngramSpark invited me to participate in their Pro publishing program.
- The book marketing expert section of the IngramSpark website features my business.

And better than any award or recognition I received? My mother flew out to Nashville one year after that fateful visit. My sister had shared what I had been going through, and mom wanted to see me. In all honesty, I was taken aback, even more so by the fact that my alters did not object. So, this time when my mom came to town, she stayed in my home, and we had a candid conversation about the past. I questioned her about timelines, people, and places that validated the details of my nightmares.

I also asked what she did to make my alters hate her so much. She told me what happened at my ninth birthday party. It wasn't anything terrible or outlandish; the guests were unaware that anything was going on. But it was horrifying for the little girl desperate for the love and affection of her mother. I believe an alter was created that day because my mom confided that I was never the same after that incident.

Our mom apologized; and Tasha, the little girl alter traumatized at her ninth birthday party, felt what we have all been searching to feel—safe.

In 2011, Elona became a passionate advocate for the Rape, Abuse, Incest National Network (RAINN). Following the publication of her memoir in 2016, she was propelled into the public eye as a #metoo activist, sharing her story, inspiring others to speak their truth, and even testifying before Congress.

Building upon her advocacy work and the success of her memoir, Elona has become a sought-after speaker and thought leader, and recently founded the award-winning indie publishing company, The Author's Journey.

Visit https://theauthorsjourney.co.

REFLECTION QUESTIONS

1. How does the author's experience challenge or support your understanding of the relationship between childhood trauma and adult mental health? Specifically, consider the concept of 'repetition compulsion.'

REFLECTION QUESTIONS

2. How does the author's workplace experience illustrate the potential impact of mental health struggles on professional life? What does this suggest about the importance of mental health awareness, professional support, and intervention in mental health crises?

REFLECTION QUESTIONS

3. Discuss the significance of the author's house purchase in relation to her search for safety. How might creating a physical safe space relate to psychological healing?

Chapter 9 | Dr. Azuré Smith-Swan

Ascending the Staircase
The Therapist in the Chair

> *Sometimes when you're in a dark place you think you've been buried, but you've actually been planted.*
>
> —Christine Caine

THE THREADS THAT BIND US

I sit with a tightness in my chest, a feeling that's become all too familiar. The weight of unspoken trauma, the echoes of pain that reverberate through generations. This is the thread that binds my story to so many others, a tapestry woven from the shared experiences of those who have their experiences with mental illness.

As I sit across from my client, listening to their story of trauma, I feel that tightness intensify — the same sensation that overwhelms me when I'm the one in the therapy chair and the very feeling that consumed me when an abusive partner's hands were wrapped around my throat. The lines between therapist, client, and survivor blurred at that moment, reminding me of the intricate tapestry of pain, resilience, and healing that unites us all.

THE ECHOES OF UNADDRESSED TRAUMA

Growing up, I witnessed the impact of unaddressed trauma in my family, but as a child, I lacked the vocabulary to name what I saw. It wasn't until years later that I could finally put names to the pain that had permeated our lives: depression, anxiety, and trauma. My parents, immigrants from Bermuda, were young when they had me — just 19 and 20. But they didn't seem "young" to me. They had grown up quickly and carried the weight of so much responsibility on their shoulders, which only intensified when they started their own family. On the surface, everything looked picture-perfect. My mother was always on the go, "ripping and running" from one activity to the next. She wore her accomplishments like armor, never slowing down for fear that the cracks in her façade would show. She filled her schedule to the brim, achieving and accomplishing as if the accolades could fill the void inside her and prove her worth to the world.

On the other hand, my father was the epitome of the firm, silent type. He worked tirelessly to provide for our family, always putting our needs before his own. He seemed unflappable like nothing could ever phase him. But I realize now that this was his way of coping. Behind closed doors, the weight of unaddressed stress and trauma took its toll. I remember hearing my parents argue when they thought I was asleep one evening. My mother's usually strong and assured voice trembled as she spoke of the exhaustion consuming her. "I'm tired of this!" she said. "I feel like I'm drowning." My father's response was silence, then a heavy sigh.

It wasn't until I became a therapist that I understood what I was witnessing. Depression and anxiety can present differently in men and women, particularly in the Black community. What we perceive as anger, irritability, or even aloofness in Black men is often a manifestation of deep emotional pain. My father's workaholism, anger, and irritability were his ways of expressing the depression and anxiety he had never learned to name. For my mother, the constant busyness was her way of outrunning the pain and proving her worth in a world that had always questioned it. Her accomplishments were a balm to the wounds of her past, but they were also a burden, a weight that she carried alone. The weight of unaddressed trauma took its toll. Anger and irritability simmered beneath the surface, ready to boil over at the slightest provocation. Anxiety raced through our veins, a constant companion that left us on edge and restless. And then there were the autoimmune disorders, the physical manifestations of the stress and trauma that had been passed down through generations.

AWAKENING TO THE CYCLE

As a child, I shouldn't have had to bear witness to certain situations. I shouldn't have had to witness the pain on my mother's face when she believed no one was looking or sense the heaviness in my father's silence. However, those memories remain indelible in my mind, serving as a constant reminder of the toll that unresolved trauma can have on a family. What I understand now is that my parents were doing the best they could with the tools they had. They were striving to break the cycles of poverty and trauma they had experienced, aiming to provide me with a better life than their own. But in doing so, they unknowingly passed down a different legacy — the legacy of unspoken pain and wounds that fester beneath the surface. It's a legacy that is all too common in the Black community, where the stigma around mental health is still so strong. We learn to maintain our strength, persevere, and never display weakness. But that strength can be a double-edged sword, cutting us from the support and resources we need to heal.

Growing up, I knew something wasn't right, but I didn't have the words to express it. It wasn't until I embarked on my journey of self-discovery and began studying social work that I started to understand the depth of what I had witnessed. In one of my classes, we discussed the concept of intergenerational trauma. The professor's explanation of the transmission of unresolved trauma from parent to child struck a chord with me. I saw echoes of my family's struggles in the stories of my friends and classmates, and I realized that we were not alone in our pain.

BREAKING FREE AND BREAKING THROUGH

I would always tell myself, "That could never be me." I convinced myself that I could outrun the trauma and break free from the cycle of pain that had ensnared my family for generations. But trauma has a way of catching up with you, no matter how fast you run. As I dove deeper into my studies and began my work as a therapist, I came face-to-face with my own wounds. I remember one client, a young woman who had experienced trauma. As she shared her story, my chest tightened, and my breath quickened. It was a visceral reminder that I had not escaped unscathed. By acknowledging my own pain, I could start my process of breaking free.

Leaving the strict household I had grown up in, I struggled to find my place in the world. In high school, I coasted by doing the bare minimum. But in college, something shifted. For the first time, I had control over my own path. I threw myself into my studies, excelling in ways that surprised even me. As I walked across the stage on graduation day, magna cum laude, and a year early, I felt a mix of emotions — surprise at how far I had come, but also a sense that this was always within me. But even as I excelled academically, I still grappled with the emotional toll of my past. Each time I visited home or called my parents, I found myself sharing new insights about mental health and the importance of addressing it. At first, these conversations felt awkward and uncomfortable. But slowly, something began to shift.

One day, while saying goodbye to my parents, I found myself uttering three words that had always felt too vulnerable: "I love you." There was a moment of silence, a hesitation that felt like an eternity. But then my parents said it back. It was a small step, but it felt like a giant leap toward breaking the generational curses that had plagued our family. Over time, those three words became a regular part of our conversations. My parents even started saying it first, wrapping me in hugs that felt like heaven. I was proud of our progress and how I was helping to shift our family history's narrative. But even as I celebrated those victories, I fell into familiar patterns. Like my mother, I filled my plate to the brim, always on the go, never slowing down. I ignored the signs of burnout, relentlessly striving for success as if my value depended on my output.

I remember one particularly challenging period during my graduate studies. I juggled a full course load, an unpaid practicum, and a full-time job. I slept four hours a night, fueling myself with coffee and adrenaline. Anger and irritability became my constant companions, a "bad attitude" that I couldn't shake. Anxiety coursed through my veins, leaving me restless and on edge. I knew something had to change, but I needed to figure out where to start.

THE PRICE OF PURPOSE

As I navigated my way through school, I found myself immersed in a field that seemed to glorify the idea of self-sacrifice. The social work profession, known for its commitment to helping others, often came with a heavy price tag, measured in long hours, low pay, and emotional exhaustion. From the beginning, we were told to prepare for a life of financial struggle and burnout. I remember one professor saying, "If you're in this for the money, you're in the wrong field." The design of our practicums mimicked the demanding schedules of full-time employees, disregarding our personal well-being. The message was clear: if you wanted to make a difference in the world, you had to be willing to give everything, even if it meant neglecting your needs.

Preaching Without Practice

It wasn't until I found myself leading group therapy sessions at the psychiatric hospital that I had a startling realization. As I stood in front of the room, teaching clients about coping skills and self-care, I suddenly realized that I had no idea how to practice those things myself. I remember one client, a middle-aged man, looking at me with a quizzical expression. "Do you actually do any of this stuff?" he asked. "Or are you just telling us to do it?" His words struck a chord. The words felt hollow in my mouth. I was preaching a sermon to a congregation without fully understanding the message myself.

Transference and countertransference were palpable as I saw echoes of my experiences in my clients' struggles and triumphs. I began to question my healing journey, wondering how I could help others heal while I was still grappling with my own wounds. Shame and confusion washed over me. I had always believed that to be an effective therapist, I had to be perfect — a shining example of mental health and stability. But as I stood in front of that room, I realized that my humanity was a strength, allowing me to connect with clients on a deeper level and model the skills I was teaching while maintaining professional boundaries.

Despite this newfound awareness, I struggled to prioritize my needs. When we learned about compartmentalization in school, I latched onto the concept like a lifeline. I convinced myself that I could neatly separate my emotions and experiences from those of my clients, tucking them away in tidy boxes until I had the time and space to deal with them. I remember one particularly challenging case: a client who had experienced severe abuse. As she shared the details of her trauma, I felt my own memories resurfacing. After the session, I was in the bathroom, shaking and fighting back tears. But I didn't allow myself to process those emotions. I splashed water on my face, took a deep breath, and moved on to my next client. But compartmentalization can only take you so far. Eventually, the boxes begin to overflow, spilling out into every aspect of your life. The constant effort of trying to please everyone depleted my emotional reserves, causing me to burn out.

Burnout crept in, manifesting in long hours, low pay, and emotional exhaustion. Key signs included constant exhaustion and irritability, difficulty disconnecting from work, and neglecting personal relationships and self-care.

BECOMING THE CLIENT

As I stepped into my new role as a licensed master social worker, I thought I had finally arrived at my destination. Little did I know that the journey was far from over and that the challenges ahead would test me in ways I never imagined. A month before the COVID-19 pandemic hit, I was riding high on accomplishing my hard-earned degree and license. Job offers were coming in, and I was finally on the path to making a difference. Then the pandemic struck, and everything changed. Job offers were rescinded. Codependency was the foundation of toxic friendships and relationships. Oh, not to mention a baby. Abuse, in all its subtle forms, stealthily entered my life. The very things I had sworn would never happen to me were happening. My ex-partner criticized me, using my profession as leverage against me. "How are you a therapist who can't even regulate their own emotions?" they sneered. "What a horrible therapist you are. You're a hypocrite."

Those words cut deep, and I found myself believing them. I also had physical cuts and bruises that were ugly reminders of what I experienced daily. I threw myself into my work, clinical training, higher licensure, and a doctoral program, desperate to escape the things that were consuming me. But there was no escape. In every session, I found myself revisiting my own pain and then immediately shoving it down to be present for my clients.

The Healing Power of Vulnerability

I had always thought of myself as a "generational curse breaker"-someone who would break free from the patterns of trauma and pain that had plagued my family for so long. But now, I felt like I was perpetuating those very same curses. The thought of my daughter going through the same struggles, the same feelings of "it could never be me," only to have it happen to her, was devastating.

In my desperation, I reached out to colleagues and clinical supervisors for support and guidance. I remember one conversation with two fellow therapists. We had a long, heartfelt discussion about the importance of self-care, setting healthy boundaries, cultivating resilience, and showing up authentically in our personal and professional lives. They shared their journeys of healing and growth, emphasizing that it's an ongoing process that requires patience, compassion, and commitment. Their words were a balm to my wounded soul, reminding me that seeking help did not make me an imposter but a courageous human being doing the necessary work to break cycles and create change. They encouraged me to prioritize my well-being, set boundaries that honor my needs, and trust in the power of vulnerability and authenticity. This conversation was a turning point, a reminder that I was not alone in my struggles and that there was wisdom and support within my community.

Their words gave me the courage to take the next step: becoming a client myself. I found myself sitting in the very chair I had sat across from so many times, but this time was different. I was finally seeking help. It was a humbling experience, and I had to fight the urge to intellectualize everything or try to predict what assessment or diagnosis I would receive.

As I allowed myself to be transparent about my own struggles, I began to see things in a new light. I remember the moment my therapist said the words, "You have depression, anxiety, ADHD, and complex PTSD." The labels felt heavy at first, like a weight I had been carrying without realizing it. But they also brought clarity and validation. I wasn't broken or flawed — I was a human being who had experienced trauma and was learning to process it and cope.

Embracing Holistic Healing

Through my journey, I've discovered effective strategies for combating burnout, including setting boundaries between work and personal life, engaging in self-care, seeking support from supervisors and a therapist, and advocating for systemic changes in the workplace.

Through trauma-informed and trauma-focused therapy, I addressed the root of my pain rather than just the symptoms. Cognitive behavioral therapy helped me to recognize and challenge the distorted thoughts that had become so automatic. I remember one session where my therapist had me write down all of my negative self-talk. Seeing the words on paper was a revelation. "Would you ever say these things to a loved one or a client?" my therapist asked. "Then why do you say them to yourself?" It was a moment of profound realization.

Dialectical behavioral therapy gave me tools to regulate my emotions, communicate more effectively, and be more present. I remember feeling a sense of control for the first time in a long time. Eye Movement Desensitization and Reprocessing therapy was a game-changer. As I processed my trauma, I could feel the power of those memories starting to dissipate. As I followed my therapist's fingers back and forth, back and forth, I felt the emotion rising in my chest. But then something shifted. The memory didn't disappear, but it lost its hold on me. It became just another part of my story, not the defining feature.

I was then introduced to the concept of holistic wellness, which included addressing the physical, energetic, mental/emotional, spiritual, and communal layers of myself. I started practicing yoga, moving my body in ways that felt nurturing. My responsibilities made it difficult to attend in-person classes on a regular basis, but I stopped making excuses and followed guided videos and books. I also became more intentional about my nutrition. Breathwork became a daily practice to regulate my nervous system, help move stagnant energy, and balance my chakras. I learned that different breathing patterns could have different effects — that I could use my breath to energize or soothe, depending on what I needed. Affirmations and therapy sessions gave me the opportunity to process thoughts and emotions and affirm myself. Spiritually, I explored my relationship with myself, God, and the universe, recognizing there was something greater than myself.

Most importantly, I prioritized my communal layer by surrounding myself with a supportive, positive community instead of isolating myself, which made me more vulnerable to experiencing trauma in the past. I started talking to and hanging out more with my trusted friends and colleagues. I even began participating in a therapist support group, where I found acceptance in all aspects of my identity. We laughed, cried, and reminded each other of our inherent worth and strength.

Our shared experiences also highlighted broader issues within the mental health field:

- The need for systemic changes to prevent burnout.
- The importance of culturally competent care addressing generational trauma.
- The power of vulnerability, transparency, and authenticity in breaking stigma.

THE POWER IN OUR STORIES

Addressing my well-being holistically was so profoundly beneficial that I decided to pursue certification to help others heal in a comprehensive way and shift my clinical approach. I'm proud to be a therapist in therapy myself, showing up more presently for myself, my loved ones, my clients, and the generations to come.

It's more than okay to be the client. To be the therapist who openly has personal lived experiences that mirror what clients face. We have endured trauma ourselves because it empowers us to change the narrative. We can rewrite our stories into ones of empowerment, resilience, and healing. We can use our voices to break stigma and generational cycles.

For those who may be struggling, know that you are not alone. Your experiences are valid, and healing is possible. It takes courage to seek help, to advocate for yourself, to sit with the discomfort, and to do the work, but it is worth it. You are worth it. People can heal from deep wounds with various evidence-based treatments that can help process and cope with trauma. However, healing is not one-size-fits-all. What works for one may not work for another, and that's okay. Surround yourself with supportive people, whether a therapist, support group or trusted friends and family. Prioritize self-care as a necessity, not a luxury. Be kind to yourself and remember that healing is not linear. Trauma can make you feel powerless, but you have agency in your journey. You are the expert in your experience, and your voice matters. You are the expert in your own experience, and your voice and needs matter. Healing is not about "fixing" or "curing" you but rather about empowering you to reclaim your sense of safety, trust, and control. It's about learning to trust your wisdom, cultivate self-compassion, and practice self-care. The process can be challenging, with good and bad days, steps forward and back. But every step, no matter how small, is a step in the right direction.

As a Black therapist, I understand the unique challenges that come with seeking mental health care in our community. The stigma, lack of access, and cultural barriers are all genuine obstacles. But they are not insurmountable. Resources and organizations dedicated to providing culturally competent care exist. Beyond the practical resources, there is also the power of community. We heal best when we heal together, when we can share our stories and our struggles, and when we can lean on each other for support. This is why I believe so strongly in the power of safe spaces where we can come together and witness each other's journeys. In my own journey of healing, it was the support of my community that made all the difference. It was the women around me, personally and professionally, who held me up when I felt like I couldn't go on. It was the elders in my life who reminded me of my strength and my ancestral resilience. My friends checked in, listened without judgment, celebrated my victories, and mourned my losses. And it is this community that I want to build for others — a community of healing and hope because we are not meant to walk this path alone.

As I continue this lifelong journey of healing and growth, I keep coming back to the beginning — to that feeling of my chest tightening as I sat across from my client, our shared trauma binding us together in an unspoken understanding of pain and perseverance. But also of hope and transformation. This is the power inherent in the work we do as therapists. Whether we're the ones in the chair or not, we're all just humans trying to make sense of this complex, messy, beautiful thing we call "life".

Reflecting on my journey brings to mind one of my mother's favorite poems, "Mother to Son" by Langston Hughes. The poem was so dear to her that she taught it to me at a young age, encouraging me to memorize it. At the time, I didn't fully grasp the profound meaning behind the words. But now, as I navigate my path of healing and growth, the poem's message of resilience and perseverance resonates with me on a deeper level. It feels like a full-circle moment, recognizing the parallels between the poem and the lives my family has lived — the generational trauma we've endured and the strength and determination we've demonstrated in the face of adversity. Like the mother in the poem, my mother's love and wisdom have been a guiding light, reminding me to keep climbing, to push through the splinters and tacks, and never give up on my journey to wholeness and healing.

We possess incredible resilience, born of struggle, pain, and the courage to keep going when the path ahead is unclear. This resilience is not a measure of how much we can endure but a testament to our inherent worth and the strength we've developed in the face of adversity. It allows us to show up each day and engage in the hard work of healing, even when it feels impossible.

As I continue my healing journey, I am committed to honoring the process, practicing self-compassion, and embracing my authentic self. I'll keep showing up and doing the work within myself and my community, striving to be a more present and grounded mother, daughter, friend, and clinician, extending the same understanding to myself that I offer to my clients. This journey is about progress, not perfection or reaching a specific destination. It's about honoring the progress we make, celebrating small victories, recognizing our strengths, and trusting in our capacity to thrive with support and self-compassion.

Dr. Azuré Smith-Swan, LCSW, CFSW

Dr. Azuré Smith-Swan, LCSW, CFSW, is a Licensed Clinical Social Worker and psychotherapist at the forefront of integrating wellness and trauma-informed care into social work. Holding a Doctorate in Social Work, she epitomizes a commitment to a holistic approach to mental wellness. Her rich background spans private practice, therapy in both inpatient and outpatient settings, nonprofits, and educational institutions, bringing a comprehensive and innovative approach to tackling modern mental health challenges.

Her professional and academic research underscores her role as a thought leader in addressing the nuances of contemporary mental health issues. As an expert mental health consultant and advisory board member, Dr. Smith-Swan has been instrumental in guiding mental health strategies, fostering community engagement, and advocating for progressive, accessible mental health care. Dr. Smith-Swan's dedication to the evolution of mental health care practices and her holistic approach to therapy mark her as a pivotal figure in the fields of social work and mental health advocacy.

https://www.linkedin.com/in/azure-smith-swan/

REFLECTION QUESTIONS

1. The author's story highlights the importance of addressing intergenerational trauma. Reflect on your own family history. In what ways might unspoken pain or unresolved trauma be impacting your life and mental well-being? What steps can you take to break free from trauma cycles and start your healing journey?

REFLECTION QUESTIONS

2. The author's experiences illustrate the challenges of being a mental health professional while navigating personal trauma and the importance of seeking help. Do you harbor any stigmas or beliefs that might prevent you from reaching out for help? What would it look like to extend the same compassion you offer others to yourself?

REFLECTION QUESTIONS

3. Throughout her journey, the author emphasizes the power of vulnerability, community support, and holistic healing practices in fostering resilience. How can you cultivate a network of supportive individuals who uplift and encourage you? What holistic healing modalities resonate with you, and how can you incorporate them into your life?

National Helplines and Resources

Helplines

988 Suicide and Crisis Lifeline: 988 or Lifeline Chat

Crisis Text Line: Text HOME TO 741741

National Domestic Violence Hotline: 800-799-7233

STAND! For Families Free of Violence Crisis Line: 888-215-5555

Childhelp National Child Abuse Hotline: 800-422-4453

Darkness to Light Child Sexual Abuse National Helpline: 866-367-5444

Stop It Now! Prevent Child Sexual Abuse Helpline: 888-PREVENT

National Center for Missing and Exploited Children Hotline: 800-843-5678

RAINN National Sexual Assault Hotline: 800-656- 4673

SAMHSA: 800-662-HELP (800-662-4357)

Partnership to End Addiction: 855-378-4373 or text CONNECT to 55753 to get one-on-one help to address your child's substance use

CHADD: 866-200-8098

Veterans Crisis Line: 800-273-8255 (Press 1)

Online Resources

BetterHelp (https://www.betterhelp.com/) – Online portal providing access to licensed therapists.

Talkspace (https://www.talkspace.com/) – Online therapy with mental health professionals.

Therapy For Black Girls (https://therapyforblackgirls.com/) – Online space dedicated to encouraging the mental wellness of Black women and girls.

Black Female Therapists (https://www.blackfemaletherapists.com/) – Offering options to support you on your mental health journey.

Mental Health America(https://www.mhanational.org/) – Resource for finding local mental health resources and support.

Support Groups

Anxiety and Depression Association of America (https://adaa.org/) – Offers support groups and resources for anxiety and depression.

PTSD Alliance (http://www.ptsdalliance.org/) – Information and resources for PTSD support.

Black Bear Lodge (https://blackbearrehab.com/mental-health/ptsd/women-veterans-and-ptsd/ – Counseling for women veterans to address PTSD.

LGBTQ+ Crisis/Suicide Prevention Hotlines

<u>Transgender Community</u>

Trans Lifeline - 877-565-8860

LGBTQ+ Youth

LGBT National Youth Talkline - 1-800-246-7743

TrevorLifeline - 1-866-488-7386

TrevorText - Text START to 678-678

The Steve Fund Crisis Textline* - Text STEVE to 741741

<u>LGBTQ+ Adults</u>

Lifeline* - 1-800-273-8255

Crisis Text Line* - Text HOME to 741741

<u>All Ages</u>

LGBT National Hotline - 1-888-843-4564

Let's Stay in Touch

Looking for more self-help reads?

The Author's Journey is an award-winning hybrid publishing company and a member of IngramSpark's prestigious Pro Program.

We publish nonfiction books and anthologies penned by industry thought leaders covering a wide range of topics.

Visit and connect with us at:

https://theauthorsjourney.co/books

www.linkedin.com/in/elonawashington

www.ingramcontent.com/pod-product-compliance
Lightning Source LLC
Chambersburg PA
CBHW050334010526
44119CB00004B/146